Earth Medicine
AND
Healing Stones

Earth Medicine
AND
Healing Stones

PRACTICES FOR HEALTH
WEALTH & LONGEVITY

Carollanne Crichton

Konecky&Konecky

Konecky & Konecky

72 Ayers Point Rd.

Old Saybrook, CT 06475

ISBN: 1-56852-572-9

Printed in China

CONTENTS

AN AFFIRMATION FOR THE EARTH

In the awareness that our Earth is eternally responsive,
may I choose right action and wisdom today.

May I choose to cherish the Earth in my stewardship of it,
so that it may continue to be the source of all vitality.

May I bring my best self to this Earth,
knowing that her wholeness lies within me,
knowing that my every thought and action touch all.

In this awareness, may I claim my true power.
May I be guided to make my inner world more gentle,
harmonious and joyful, so that I may offer these
qualities back to the world and to this Earth.

May I cherish the Earth and all those with whom I share it.

In the awareness that our Earth is eternally responsive,
may I choose right action and wisdom today.

We are part of the Earth and it is part of us.

The perfumed flowers are our sisters.

The deer, the horse, the great eagle: these are our brothers.

The rocky crests, the juices of the meadows,

The body heat of the pony and man

All belong to the same family.

The Earth does not belong to man; man belongs to the Earth.

This we know. All things are connected

Like the blood which unites one family.

All things are connected.

Whatever befalls the Earth befalls the sons and daughters
of the Earth.

Man did not weave the web of life; he is merely a strand in it.

Whatever he does to the web, he does to himself.

—CHIEF SEATTLE

REAWAKENING
OUR INDIGENOUS MIND

SOMEWHERE along the way of progress, we have rearranged our priorities. We have allowed societal values, many of which defy the wellbeing of our bodies and that of the planet, to override our inner promptings and innate wisdom. Our relationship to the earth is one-sided: disposable consumerism and lack of concern for preservation of natural resources reflect the notion that we can exploit the earth indefinitely. Our elders no longer remember the stories of their ancestors, nor do they guide us in the circle of giving and receiving that lifts a life from raw materiality to one of purpose and meaning.

And yet a revival of ancient wisdom connecting us to a deeper relationship with the earth is upon us. Indigenous peoples not exposed to the civilizing influences of the West have modes of perception and sensing that keep them in touch with the nonhuman as well as the human world.

That innate sensibility was apparent in the Andaman Islands of Southeast Asia in the weeks following the cataclysmic tsunami of 2005. After hopes had been dashed that there were any additional survivors of the deadly waves which already had claimed more than 200,000 lives in the region, rescue teams were astounded to discover that native islanders had not suffered any fatalities. This remote tribe had its own information technology: powered by gut instinct and myth, they had paid close attention to the rapid retreat of a huge volume of sea water. To their way of understanding, this represented a displeased deity in the form of the ocean, and their ocean deity was so angry that they knew its return would be with great fury. They immediately fled to hide in the hills and later emerged unharmed.

We, too, are inherently endowed with these same sensibilities but have allowed them to atrophy, forgetting the profound interdependence of all living things in the earth community.

To recover the dormant indigenous mind requires a steady *open*-mindedness, for it goes against mores cultivated over time which guide us to disavow and exclude these ways of knowing and being. The split from our own natural selves has caused us to become destructive to ourselves, to each other, and to the natural world—for the most part unwittingly, although the consequences are now becoming clear.

Inertia is always tough to interrupt, yet if these sensibilities can be restored we may consciously and creatively bring about changes that will assist the soul of our culture and planet, in recovery and reawakening.

Earth medicine finds soul in all things. It sees the physical body as the natural extension of soul, both personal and collective. Just as unseen atoms unite to form molecules that combine to build matter, so the invisible soul is made manifest and conveyed to us through symptoms of disease and malaise. Long ago, descriptions of bodily tissues and their functions were communicated by way of simple elemental images found in nature. When understood this way, illness reports to us about the soul, the psyche, and the body.

The sensibility of indigenous medicine reflects all life processes in this way, while modern medicine functions as a biomedical science favoring fragmentation over wholeness, matter over spirit. The emotional, spiritual, and soulful aspects of healing are often neglected.

As a science, modern medicine has come far in the care of the human body through analysis, research, and practice, yet it often ignores the traditional healing arts developed prior to the rise of the scientific method. Although some individual physicians have tried to include alternative methods with standard medical practice, most members of the medical profession have kept these practices separate from "scientific" medical care. In particular, modern medicine generally avoids herbalism, mineralogy, subtle energy therapies, and the mind-body-spirit relationship. Nonetheless, more and more individuals find greater meaning and quality of life through the inclusion of sacred rituals and practices from the distant past.

This book reverently explores the healing power of earth's natural forces, sharing treasured philosophies, mythological perspectives, and indigenous earth cures that may help us tap directly into vital resources for health, prosperity, and inner peace. Many of the earth cures center on the energies found in non-precious stones, rocks, and clays; but overall they represent a way of rediscovering the sacred relationship with the earth that has sustained and nurtured mankind for thousands of years. In many cases they simply ask us to use the common sense that we dismiss or overlook in our hurried lives.

Ideas alone are not enough to create a whole life, or to heal the earth. Information does not necessarily lead to transformation. For transformation, or in order to embrace information as truth, the psyche and the body need internal, personal experience.

For this reason, there are many personal, inner practices in this book. For example, in Chapter 4 you will find a four-week program integrating diet, exercise, and rejuvenating healing arts. If you or a family member has a specific physical health goal in mind such as weight loss, increased energy, or increased strength and stamina, you will find ways to tailor the program to those needs. For further support in weight loss and detoxification, An appendix offers step-by-step guidance in the use of healing clays for purification and elimination of toxins. If you are interested in the spiritual roots of wealth, financial stability and societal interdependence, Chapter 6 on *Artha Vidya*, may be a great reference to bookmark.

For massage practitioners: you will discover here a comprehensive study of the art and science of stone massage culled from decades of hands-on experience and research. This portion of the book, covering information critical to giving a healing stone massage safely and effectively, could stand alone as an adjunct to other types of professional massage training. It will also be of practical value for non-professionals who are interested in sharing massage with loved ones.

More than singling out any one practice or remedy however, this book is meant to inspire. It is an offering for the soul, intended to reunite your soul with the great spirit moving within and around us on earth. Choose the practices or exercises that you feel most drawn to and pass the others on.

CHAPTER ONE

LIFE IN THE 21ST CENTURY: THE AGE OF ZERO GRAVITY

Man is an over-complicated organism.
If he is doomed to extinction,
He will die out for wanting simplicity.
—EZRA POUND

HAVE YOU EVER climbed a tree in New York's Central Park? Can you smell the sea on the air in Los Angeles? Do you feel the ebb and flow of great tides in Chicago? To many people, if they think about it at all, the trees along city streets seem to grow miraculously out of asphalt and concrete—or seem to be mere stopping places for dogs. Many of us live governed by daily routines that disengage us from the rhythms of the natural universe. We have very little education in nature. We are held back by custom and familiarity—far away from our senses and the appetites of the soul.

Our modern cities, made of glass and concrete towers, express civilization's ceaseless urge to reach beyond survival. Our collective eyes are lifted skyward; the vastness of space is full of potential beyond the towers on the ground. All large cities, with their institutions of art and culture gesturing toward integration and wholeness, seem unwittingly to foster the notion that humanity is separate from nature. Somewhere "out there" are the glaciers, forests, open seas, the earth itself.

To the indigenous mind, this split between city and nature illustrates the predicament of modern life, from which, to their way of thinking, the deities have been banished.

Troublesome symptoms of this estrangement include urban sprawl; polluted air and water; rampant growth and expansion; and the stifling regulations and bureaucracy that now plague much of contemporary urban life. Civilized people no longer know how to survive in a natural environment:

*"Progress is the
dirtiest word
in the English
language—who
ever told us and
made us believe
it—that to take
a step forward
was necessary,
was always a
good idea?"*

—EDNA
ST VINCENT
MILLAY

most do not know how to grow the food they eat; how to find drinkable water; how to build a fire; what the sky portends and how to read it; when the growing seasons begin and end; which plants in the forest and field are safe to eat; how to track, kill, dress, cut, and store game; how to treat broken bones, reduce a fever naturally, deliver a baby, or how to handle other common medical situations.

In fact, children don't even play outside as much as they did in the past. A study done from 1970-1990 shows that the open space boundaries or radius of freedom that children have access to has been reduced by ninety percent. By favoring a technological focus and feeding fears about the "boogeyman in the woods," we deprive future generations of a sense of texture and awe regarding the real, natural world.

A recent report featured a group of young men from an inner city gang who were brought to wooded areas to help cut trails. They were terrified of the forest. They said that it was "too noisy" and that they didn't know what the noises "meant." For them the cacaphony of urban life consisted of about five predictable sounds: traffic, machinery, conversation, gunshots, and music. They knew how to interpret these sounds but were at a loss when confronted with the richness of natural life.

The good news: after a few hours spent in the woods, these young men reportedly lost their "flatline gaze" and could be seen frolicking like eight-year olds, jumping over streams.

Thanks to information technologies, we can sit before a computer monitor and relate to one another—conduct business, trade goods, and interpret any of life's processes at the speed of light. We have progressed brilliantly into the information age, but with this age of infinite data has come numbing of our instincts and dulling of our senses.

Being thus mentally focused, we end up feeling little of the physical commotion inside our bodies that our forebears did. They relied upon the full range of their senses to understand and master their environment in comparatively simpler exchanges. Progress has left our modern view of nature and of the earth somewhat simplistic, given how complex and rich it actually is.

For example, astronomers today are more apt to peer at a computer monitor than to consider the stars with their naked eyes. This is not to say that they don't continue to use their senses to interpret the data organized by the computer. In fact such information can register subtleties as a rush of fire in their eyes rising to the brain, or as a quiet, palpable settling deep within their bones.

As they patiently sit and gaze at their monitors analyzing models of space and time, modern astronomers adapt not only their empirical perception of the heavens, but their body-mind as well. An evolving species, we humans challenge our inborn nature to meet the demands of our environment. Evolution, and perhaps more importantly, awareness of our progress, is the work of the soul. This is crucial to our wellbeing and fulfillment.

Studies undertaken by NASA have reported that astronauts experiencing prolonged separation from earth will undergo modification of their physiology. This occurs in part due to the demands of zero gravity, and in part to the lack of sensory landmarks in the vastness of space. Their brains adapt at the same time as physiology reorients itself. In terms of the overload to the nervous system and other stresses in the body, walking in space may not be as far removed from the "earthlessness" of modern living as one would imagine.

When we speak of suffering from low energy levels, chronic illness, or high stress, we are describing the body's response to sensory information that is given to the brain. Scientists have estimated that the average adult thinks some fifty thousand thoughts per day. The body attempts to respond to these mes-

sages by creating neuropeptides, compounds the brain releases to communicate. These neuropeptides are read by every cell in every organ, throughout every system in the body.

The fact that sensory perception does not end as our lives become less physical and more technological, that our brains adapt at the same time that our physiology reorients itself to change, is a good thing. It provides us with healthy internal buffers to the intensity of the world we navigate daily.

As resilient and adaptable as we are, without the opportunity to

channel external stimuli in a balanced manner our nerves would fire all at once, constantly. We would have zero energy available to function. We would die. Therefore instead of numbing ourselves, it is essential to pay attention to low energy, chronic illness, and stress levels, as harbingers of change.

All beings on the planet are born with survival skills and equipment. Some have been given claws and teeth and fierce jaws. Some are endowed with camouflage, while others wear visible armor. Humans have teeth, claws, protective armor, and camouflaging skills to a certain degree, but our inherent tools are disappearing since they are not being called upon. This is due to the fact that for humans, the most powerful tool for survival is intuition.

Why do we ignore our intuition and avoid listening to our inner voice?

As children, our intuition is intact; we know what we feel. As adults we've learned to relegate our primary survival sense to a place far from view. Our intuition is hidden away as "the sixth sense," something extraordinary and rare. Learning to trust it again may well be the most important and noble effort to which we can commit as adults.

We will either evolve creatively or extinguish our inner spark of vibrancy. How well we are able to digest, integrate, and assimilate incoming sensory messages is often reflected in our physical condition. Slowing down, quieting the mind and feeling the ground beneath our feet is a good place to start in order to perceive the guidance of our inner truth. There is a saying: "What you feel you can heal."

The ancients' attitude toward healing and the earth springs from a primordial experience of being on the one hand a guest, and on the other, an offspring, of earth. The earth is undoubtedly mother, close to us; but at the same time also alien, other. Earth is our foundation, out of which emerges all that exists and upon which everything that we experience rests. The earth is the basis of life.

When considered as a divine being, earth always occupies a special place among the gods.

We are of the earth and earthly, but the earth is not simply nature, not merely geographical or material. It is part of us, so that we can no more live without the earth than we can live without a body. At the same time, though we stand on the earth we also stand above her; we are more than the earth.

This tension between humanity and earth is always present, but there is no true separation. Early cultures would find any attempt at dominating or subjugating the earth incomprehensible. The earth was an object of worship and awe, not exploitation and research. Worship of the earth is not the same as idolatory; it is not the absolute adoration of something. It is rather the veneration of the highest value in the hierarchy of existence. According to the *Vedas* (the sacred texts of India), "undoubtedly this earth is the firstborn of being." (*Rig Veda* 69). The earth is the dwelling place of all creatures and people, dispenser of all resources, and also a cosmic power. Accordingly, ecology and natural healing can be said to have been sacred sciences from the earliest times.

NATURAL HEALING

Ancient healing exercises have long offered people practical antidotes to the concept of living without a "root" or connection to the earth. These practices involve engaging a personal, internal connection with the gravity field of the earth, with the downward flow of electromagnetic energy.

There are times when we instinctively know that our bodies, brains, and nerves crave calmness and peace. We sense that the serenity we seek may be found in nature, in silence, and by turning inward. This is a basic form of healing with nature. "Natural healing" may be described as the process of returning the body and mind to a natural state, better able to integrate, digest, and assimilate life's changes.

TWO NATURAL HEALING MEDITATIONS

I. MOUNTAIN MEDITATION

This is a practice derived from Buddhist teachings. It uses the mountain as a symbol of the earth's strength. The essence of a mountain is stability, a deep and

"It is far more important that one's life should be perceived than that it should be transformed; for no sooner has it been perceived, than it transforms on its own accord."

—MAURICE MAETERINICK
THE DEEPER LIFE

abiding quality that withstands the changes of time. It is the solidity of rock and the stabilizing function of earth. In many traditions, a mountain symbolizes stillness. Serene and detached, rising above mundane affairs, it remains unaffected by the strife of the world. A mountain setting offers the perfect environment for meditation.

In human life, stability manifests as a firm footing in the present. It arises when we believe in ourselves and can focus on the task at hand. Sometimes healing requires us to put down roots, to stabilize. Going deep within can bring us to great heights.

When we simply sit—relaxing the body keeping the spine upright, closing our eyes, and shifting our attention from the outer to the inner—we may tune in to the stillness of the mountain. From this centered place it is possible to rise above the mind's busy-ness and gain a detached overview. With some distance from mental preoccupations, we are able to observe ourselves with objectivity.

PREPARATION

This meditation is both a point of rest and a process of renewal from the inside out. It arrests the driving force of compulsion.

Use this meditation practice at those times when you need to withdraw from the world and rest in "being." Without periodic retreats, it is easy to become overly identified with one's position and place in the hubbub of worldly affairs and to begin to call that "the truth." Once we start to believe that life should revolve around serving the demands of this reality, the real treasures of our being are lost. Worldly reality tells us that life's entire meaning lies in doing and acquiring. If we follow the dictates of that belief, we are taken on a long and disappointing journey; in the end, this only takes us away from our own truth.

The central point of the mountain meditation is to observe whatever is bubbling up in the mind and emotions and to let it all go. When thoughts or feelings are happy or fascinating in some way, the tendency is to grasp hold of them, to replay them, and to exclude other thoughts. On the other hand, when thoughts or feelings are disturbing or painful, the mind works quickly to suppress them, or it busies itself trying to analyze the external source of the condition. Whether your thoughts are happy or sad, the mind will want to engage them somehow. It will try working out a strategy to direct them in some way, according to its own preferences.

The mountain meditation is a way of stepping out of this pattern, a way of putting aside the preferential thinking that distracts us from living in accordance with our true inner nature. From the inner mountaintop perspective we can realize that the real treasure we seek has always been within our reach. Once we are back in touch with this essential treasure, it will be easier to withdraw from any difficulties that may be insisting upon our attention.

Meditation should not be a serious, hard-to-manage affair; rather, it is as natural as breathing, as awakening as fresh mountain air. Use the following guidelines when you are fatigued or stressed, or when problems seem too insurmountable for you to gain the strength to continue and overcome them.

TO START

Sit comfortably with your spine upright, eyes closed. Breathe slowly and deeply, but try to breathe with an inaudible breath. A silent breath reflects a silent mind.

THE PRACTICE

Imagine yourself sitting at the bottom of a mountain whose peak is hidden by clouds. You embark on the climb up toward the top of the mountain. It is a long and arduous ascent in the damp chilly air, steep and rocky, into thicker and thicker mist. You concentrate on placing one foot in front of the other, trusting that the path will eventually lead to your destination.

When distracting or tangential thoughts come to your awareness, simply focus on the path before you. As you approach the summit, see the clouds disperse and the way clear. Find a place in the clear area at the mountaintop to sit in observation of the valley below. Let the valley symbolize your life or the particular situation about which you desire perspective. Know that this is the right moment to gain an overview, to see what is needed.

Once you know that you are not a victim of circumstance but only of your own thoughts, the entire landscape begins to shift. It is as if there is more time and spaciousness. Life can be experienced as the extraordinary generosity that it is.

THE REFLECTION

Life is a gift. Once you recognize this, everything that seemed difficult becomes easy. As you emerge from the meditation, resolve to carry the stillness and serenity of the mountain with you. Remember to speak and act from inner

stillness. Watch your words and your actions now as carefully as you watched your feet on the path up the mountain to the clearing at the top: not with tension, but with care. When you move with this inner stability, you'll feel the resonance within your every word and gesture.

2. Peaceful Mind Meditation

This is a sacred meditation practice drawn from the Tantric Yoga texts for inner peace. It utilizes the imagery of water and moonlight to bring calmness and luminosity to your mental and emotional states. When the surface of a lake is still, it reflects the moon above it perfectly. But when the water is troubled, or if we drop a few pebbles into the lake, the one moon appears as many, and the bottom cannot be seen at all. A great treasure could lie there, but it will remain undiscovered until the waters above are still.

PREPARATION

Sit (or lie down) comfortably. Unplug the phone and create a space that will not be interrupted for ten to fifteen minutes.

TO START

Without effort or trying to change the way you naturally breathe, inhale and exhale fully, slowly, and deeply, in and out through your nose. Bring your breath all the way down to the lower portion of each lung and into your back. Lengthen your neck gently as you breathe in, allowing your shoulders to drop away toward the earth as you breathe out. Expand this awareness, breath by breath, so that as you inhale you feel the crown of your head as a soft space opening upward, and as you exhale you give the weight of your body over to the downward gravitational pull of the earth.

As you breathe, there is no need to pull the air in forcefully. Nor is there any benefit to be gained from pushing the air out strongly. Try to keep a silent breath rather than a noisy stream of air.

THE REFLECTION

With a softened inner gaze, imagine that the center of your brain is a lake. Observe the surface of the lake, and sense the depth of the water in this lake. Now, look on the inner surface of the back of your skull, and see a rising full moon, full of luminosity. As this moon rises, you can see its light

OPPOSITE: **Light falling on Mont Blanc**

shimmering over the entire surface of the lake, creating beauty and peace in your mind.

Follow the rays of the moon to the inside of your forehead, to a point that rests between your eyes. Allow this point to expand until you can see it opening outward.

Now, direct the rays of inner moonlight out into your energy field, which is that area surrounding your body about six inches off the surface. Take your time; there is no need to rush. Surround your physical body—front, back, sides, top and bottom—with light and peace.

Sit in the awareness and knowledge that this field of energy is magnetic and full of potential. See its energy piercing and nourishing each and every cell in your body.

Follow the light back now, into the point between your two eyes and to the center of your brain. Gather the energy of the light at the center of your brain and consolidate it into a small bead that now travels down the channel of your spine all the way to the bottom of your feet. As the bead of light travels down your spine, sweep away any accumulated tensions, toxins or negative thoughts. As you inhale, feel the entire surface of your feet; and as you exhale, release tensions, toxins or old thoughts out through your feet and into the earth, where they will be neutralized.

Finally, inhale fresh light up the spine, into the center of your brain once again.

COMPLETING THE PRACTICE

When you feel complete with the practice, gently open your eyes and return awareness to your surroundings.

Focus on the sensations that arise as your breath bridges the chasm separating body and mind. Allow yourself to become fully present in your body and more aware of the messages you may be holding for yourself.

See how this simple exercise has shifted your energy. With the calming influence of meditation, stresses in the mind and body dissolve.

The imagery of water and moonlight evokes tranquility

CHAPTER TWO

ENERGY MEDICINE: LIFE IS BUT A STREAM

All the rivers run into the sea,
Yet the sea is not full.
Unto the place
Whence the rivers come,
Thither they return again.
—ECCLESIASTES 1:7

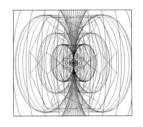

A simple model
of energy flow

PHYSICISTS TELL US that energy supercedes all matter. They tell us that matter is simply energy, vibrating at a frequency that resonates with our optic nerve in such a way that the energy appears as a solid. Given this, it makes sense that if we can harmonize the energy, the matter will take care of itself through the laws of cause and effect.

All medicinal cultures throughout the ages have recognized the fundamental principles of the vital energy within the body. The oldest medical system, Ayurveda from India, calls this vital force "prana". In traditional Chinese Medicine it is called "chi". Even the early Middle East and Western medicinal practices acknowledge the energy forces of the body. In ancient Greece it was called "pneuma". The Hebrews called it "ruach". Islamic cultures called it "baraka". And in Polynesia it is called "mana".

If energy supercedes matter, then it also makes sense that you cannot separate the vital energy sources of the body from the body. Yet today, Western medicine only treats the physical body (matter) and completely ignores the energy that directly affects the matter. That is why there is so much chronic disease in our culture: the energy that creates the condition of the matter is never addressed and healed.

Much pain and suffering could be avoided if we would address the energy fields of the body before disease is experienced.

Surrounding your body is an energy field that contains all of the information that constitutes your body, thoughts, and emotions. Likewise, the earth is surrounded by an electromagnetic field created by the ionosphere as well as the soil's composition of minerals.

Electromagnetic analysis of the minerals within earth's soils, clays, and stones reveals information that could have a profound effect not on only medicine, but on consciousness itself. Such analysis shows us that the effects of the earth's electromagnetic energy field on the body's subtle energy can produce immediate and positive responses within the body, typically associated with an increased sense of well-being, enhanced mental awareness, and clarity.

Put simply, if, on a regular basis, you put a substance into your energy field that has vital electromagnetic properties, it will take that energy and transform it into a more healthy and positive experience than if you were to repeatedly ingest negative, unhealthy, or toxic thoughts and substances.

Many people claim that they do not feel the subtle shifts in their reality but, according to hands-on healers, the dramatic effect to the etheric energy is just as profound for those who claim not to be aware of it as it is for those who are sensitive to this level of consciousness.

Indeed, earth medicine from all cultures produces a radiant (emission of light) energy within the body's cells which some researchers call the "quantum oscillation pattern." This optimal movement pattern has superconductive effects on DNA and has the potential to rejuvenate and transform, integrating life experience into a more beneficial pattern.

If we were to liken the body to a stream, we could see how it is designed to maintain perfectly coherent vitality. Its energy flows according to basic laws of physics: sourced from highest potential, running towards lowest potential, eventually returning to source, in a perpetual cycle.

A stream is drawn like a magnet toward its source, the sea. It has its own natural rhythm, natural direction of flow, and is structured for self cleansing and renewal. Although its rate, velocity, and amplitude may fluctuate in response to random thermal influences, its innate "wisdom" simply follows the parameters of a natural template. Both the water and earth elements must be in balance, with neither being excessive or depleted for a prolonged period of time.

To better understand from an energy medicine viewpoint how people get sick, envision a twig dropping into the stream. A few months later, another twig

*"The displace-
ment of a little
sand can change
the course of
deep rivers."*

—MANEUL
GONZALES

**Sahasrara, the
crown chakra**

OPPOSITE: **Tantric dia-
grams showing the
energy centers in
the hands and feet**

falls. This one jams up against the first one. There they stay, diverting the flow of water in a small way. Soon a few leaves gather, then some pebbles, and a few more leaves, and so on. In time either a new tributary forms, pulling water away from the central channel, or an acceleration of flow, a "rapid" develops. This model of circulation of energy from "greater to lesser channels" has formed the basis for many ancient healing traditions. These actions are part of the order of natural life, and as such may be relied upon to renew, restore, and self correct.

Likewise, human energy belongs to a larger system of energy. Instead of water, however, the body's energy channels contain a colorless, free-flowing, non-cellular fluid which conveys energy throughout the body. This energy is at once both spiritual and physical. Earth medicine shows us how any division between spirit and matter, even if only drawn for practical purposes, is artificial. Ancient medical texts discuss this: "For he who sees the waters only as a colorless material liquid with certain physical properties will surely fail to know what water really is. He who, on the other hand, neglects the internal physical structure and does not bother to study its properties will equally miss the point." [1]

The major energy points, channels, and centers discussed in virtually every ancient system of medicine are electromagnetic centers which function like resistors in an electrical circuit, adjusting the amplitude of energy. When body electricity, or polarity, is imbalanced, the points respond by adjusting the energy flow. If this disturbance becomes recurrent or habitual, the channel is impaired and affects the corresponding muscles, tissues, and organs.

Let's say the branch that fell into the stream symbolizes a trauma or injury. The original event may in time engrave a new pattern, just as the first branch in the stream attracted the accumulation of leaves and pebbles. Life energy may accumulate or drain away.

It is important to understand the interconnectedness between the body and the mind in relation to constitutional medicine. If, for example, a person becomes chronically agitated, driven, uptight, and tense, then the "positive" charge electromagnetic polarity circuits will overload and deprive the "negative" charge electromagnetic polarity circuits of vital energy. The body meridians are very much like a single river with tributaries flowing one into the other: if part of the river is congested and swollen by a log jam, the water level downstream slows to a trickle.

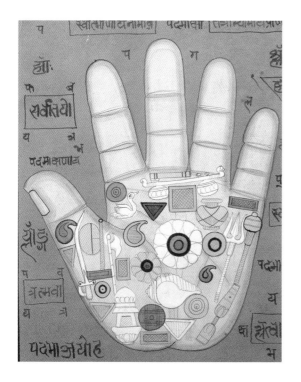

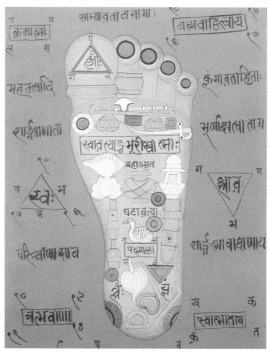

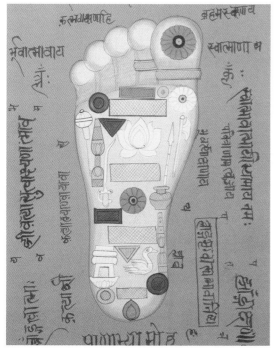

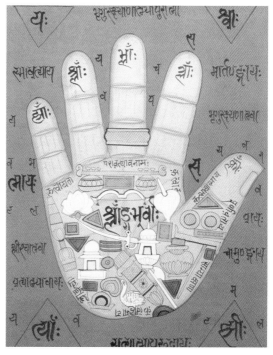

There are various systems that deal with these pathways of life force in the physical body, but the underlying principles are the same. All traditional healing methods share a common core philosophy.

In Chinese medicine, these channels are referred to as meridians. In traditional Indian medicine, there is a similar subtle energy system comprised of channels called *nadis*. Western medicine acknowledges the subtle anatomy in its acceptance of reflex zones called dermatomes.

It is important to remember that not all traditions use the same mapping system, and that in certain instances a "point" is actually more of a broadband region without precise boundaries. Almost every tradition, however, describes two primary energy storage channels running through the central body, with seven plexuses, glandular centers, or chakras that align along these two channels like transducers. Each time there is a shift in polarity, there is a shift in the core or deep energy. Disease starts with imbalanced, excessive, or suppressed energy.

The seven energy and glandular centers serve as a communication network between the physical body and vital body. According to this model, emotions, thoughts, and beliefs are translated into physical manifestations.

Individuals with sensitivity may be able to perceive the movement of this type of energy in themselves as well as in others. One way to access and interpret energy patterns is to learn how to sense variations in muscle tension. Muscular pain, stiffness, and tension are indicative of congestion and overstimulation in a related meridian or *nadi*. Muscular fatigue, weakness, and flaccidity are indicative of depletion and insufficiency.

Another way to look at the subtle energy system is by interpreting patterns of thermal radiation perceived with our hands. In energy healing it is important to develop refined sensing and hand skills in addition to other ways of receiving information. To perceive thermal patterns the hands are held near, but not necessarily touching, the skin or the clothed body. The potential for sensory acuity in humans is far greater than most people realize, although the conditions of modern civilization discourage most of us from reaching that potential.

Interpreting this information may reveal the localization of pathology in the body, or in the soul, and is the subject of numerous excellent books for further study. However, within the scope of this book it is impossible to say precisely which organ governs a particular emotional behavior, or that by simply feeling heat or energy at the point or center in question we can accurately characterize the severity of a lesion, an inflammation, or a blockage. Sensation intensity

"That the sky is brighter than the earth means little unless the earth itself is appreciated and enjoyed. Its beauty loved gives it the right to aspire to the radiance of the sunrise and the stars."

—HELEN KELLER
MY RELIGION

may well be greater for a minor joint inflammation than for a more serious injury. It is necessary to be aware of the limitations of intuitive diagnosis without proper medical training.

The phenomenon of hands-on healing with energy has been recognized for thousands of years. Dr. Bruno Roche of Geneva attributes the earliest known energy-based thermal diagnosis in medicine to Hippocrates, who is said to have covered patients with mud. Noting the places where the mud dried most rapidly, Hippocrates found that these were typically the sites of medical problems. This may be due to the fact that all tissues and functions, including the emotions, give rise to characteristic thermal or energetic flows when they are disrupted.

Energy equilibrium of an organ or muscle depends largely upon the capacity of blood and electromagnetic energy to enter and pass through. "Blocked" energy flow reduces blood circulation in the corresponding physical location, causing localized vasoconstriction. Heat or energy loss from an internal organ is a function of the quantity of blood passing through it as well as of the tone of the surrounding blood vessels. A decrease in blood flow weakens tissue, priming the affected area for injury or disease.

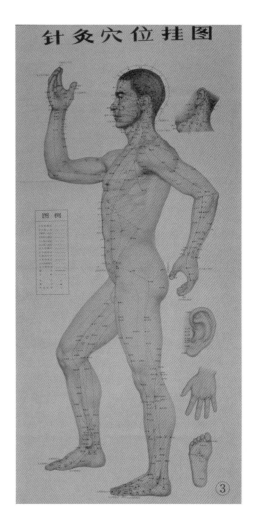

The meridian system according to the teachings of acupuncture.

Opening and clearing energy channels maintains circulation and renews the blood supply, encouraging a return to health.

Some of the points, centers, and channels of the ancient healing traditions are taught as bridging inner and outer consciousness, connecting us to environmental and universal flows of energy. For instance, upward rising and downward flowing energy channels, the "central" and "governing" channels in Chinese meridian theory, may be seen as plugging us into heaven and earth forces. Likewise, in the native medicines of the Americas, upward flowing pathways of energy are referred to as antennae to the Great Spirit. In yogic science the point on the top of the head is called the "Lord of All" point, where individual consciousness merges with universal consciousness in meditation. Also, from

Ayurveda, we learn that the energetic region at the top of the head extends off of the physical body; it is referred to as the "Crown Chakra" or "Cosmic Consciousness Chakra."

EXERCISE FOR ENERGIZING THE BODY: BRIDGING HEAVEN AND EARTH

This exercise is drawn from yogic practices for increasing spiritual and physical vitality.

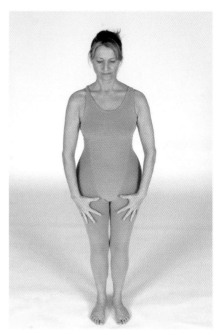

Step 1

Stand erect with hands on the thighs, fingers spread.

1. Take a deep inhalation through the nose. Circle the arms out and bring hands together in the prayer position at the heart. Exhale through the mouth.

2. Inhale through the nose while separating the hands: one arm stretches straight above the head with the palm facing up toward heaven; the other arm stretches straight down your side with the palm facing toward the earth.

3. Visualize that you are drawing heaven's force down into your body and into the earth through your palms. Retain your inhalation for three to five beats in this position. Exhale, still in this position, and retain the breath out for three to five beats.

LEFT: **Step 2**

4. Breathe in, and return your hands to the prayer position.

5. Repeat the practice, alternating arms, doing as many repetitions as desired.

6. Complete the practice by letting both arms rest by your sides and allowing your body to bend forward at the waist, in a forward fold. Feel free to bend your knees. Take two or three deep breaths.

7. Slowly roll back up to standing, stacking the vertebrae one at a time. End with shoulder rolls forward and backward.

Step 6

Bodily points of access to the strengthening, vital forces within the earth are mapped out as well. Points at the bottoms of the feet are known in Chinese medicine as "Bubbling (or Gushing) Spring." This is an image meant to assist us in feeling the natural movement of the earth's energy through the soles of the feet rising up inside the center of each leg, bubbling with vital essence like a spring.

BUBBLING SPRING ENERGY CULTIVATION

This practice, adapted from ancient Taoist internal energy cultivation methods, can be done on a daily basis. It effectively opens up the energy lines of the body, expels toxic and stagnant energies, and stimulates fresh energy to flow through the channels and joints. It utilizes the imagery of the inner earth, with the rising energy of a bubbling spring replenishing the kidney channel. It can be done in as little as five minutes for a quick boost.

Stand erect. Rub your hands together to create some friction and heat. Close your eyes.

1. When your hands are warm, rub your kidney area and then lay the hands in place, covering the kidneys.
2. Imagine that there is a line, or a light, inside the body, connecting the kidneys to the soles of your feet. Drop that line from the feet deep into the ground below you. Be aware of the adrenal glands; bring the light into the adrenal glands as well as the kidneys.
3. Feel the softness of the earth as if it were late spring and the ground were warming. Your feet are making a slight impression into the ground; feel the energy within the earth coming up through your soles like a bubbling spring. The more you feel the bubbling spring, the more it charges your kidneys.
4. Once the kidneys become fully charged, draw the energy up to your crown and mid-eyebrow region. Continue to feel energy pulsing in your palms and the soles of your feet.
5. When the energy becomes more full in the center of the brain, allow it to stream throughout your entire body swiftly and strongly. Feel every single cell in the body absorbing this energy.
6. Feel every cell having much more interconnection now. It is like osmosis. You are glowing with inner light.

Ayurveda teaches that the lower pelvic floor region, the sitting bones, the base of the tailbone, and the soles of the feet make up what is thought of as our subtle body Root System, with the Earth Chakra (feet) and Root Chakra (sacral plexus) animating and nourishing the glands and structures located there.

Other systems use different energy models. In martial arts, for example, some potent points are known to be so physically important that they are called "death-producing," or "life-sustaining." These descriptions recognize that injury at those specific sites can drive the life out of a body.

No matter what our orientation and mapping system, the key to health is to support the potent points, keeping the channels open with a balanced energy flow so that the life force is available to nourish and enliven our physical experience.

Setting sun over partially frozen reservoir in Alberta, Canada

The cosmos according to the Tibetan teachings of Kalachakra

CHAPTER THREE

MOTHER OF THE UNIVERSE: CREATION MYTHS

Earth being so good,
Would Heaven seem best?
—ROBERT BROWNING

TO HELP BRING a sense of connection and meaning to our daily lives, a look at the symbolism and lore surrounding the creation of the earth is as important for us today as ever. Although these creation stories are thousands of years old, they are timeless and have important lessons to teach us.

There are three primary recurring themes within creation myths, most familiar to us from Judeo-Christian, Hindu, Native American, and Norse stories. A variety of deities and images is interwoven into each depiction, animating the three motifs.

1. Representations of human genesis;
2. The interconnectedness between heaven and earth;
3. How a supernatural force or divine being distills order from chaos, both in the beginning and throughout time.

This account of creation can be found in the Rig Veda:

This universe existed in darkness, unperceived, unknowable, wholly immersed, as it were, in deep sleep. Then the Divine Self appeared with irresistible power, dispelling the darkness. He who is eternal, shone forth of his own will. He, desiring to produce beings of many kinds from his own body, first with a thought created the waters, and placed his seed in them. That seed became a golden egg, in brilliance equal to the sun; in that egg he himself was born as Brahma, the progenitor of the whole world. . .The Divine One resided in that egg during a whole year, then he himself by his thought divided it into two halves; and out of those two halves he formed heaven and earth.

OVERLEAF: **Giant's**
Causeway, Ireland

Taoist philosophy suggests that the whole of existence is not a chaos but rather a cosmos of immense harmony and intrinsic order. What is above—heaven— is also below—earth. The physical rests upon the subtle.

Yin-yang is the Taoist symbol of wholeness and non-duality

> *There was something formless and perfect before the universe was born.*
>
> *It is serene. Empty. Solitary. Unchanging. Infinite. Eternally present.*
>
> *It is the mother of the universe.*
>
> *For lack of a better name, I call it Tao.*
>
> *It flows through all things, inside and outside, and returns to the origin of all things.*
>
> *The Tao is great. The universe is great. Earth is great. Man is great.*
>
> *These are the four great powers.*
>
> *Man follows the earth. Earth follows the universe.*
>
> *The universe follows the Tao.*
>
> *The Tao follows only itself.*
>
> —LAO-TZU, TAO TE CHING, BOOK OF THE WAY[1]

In studying creation mythologies we see that heaven is not viewed so much as separate from earth as it is in manifest mutual reception with it. We have learned from Chinese pictographs and texts that in ancient times heaven was understood as ultimate potential, an atmosphere of receptivity so charged that it brimmed on the point of being. Known as the dragon power, it was depicted as an illuminated dragon continuously twisting in the darkness of the void. In the West, this has been called the "Hand of God" that creates all things.

The Chinese character Qian in the *I Ching* is an image of a rising sun radiating its light and energy to initiate potential. It is interesting to note that King Wen, when writing the book, did not name Qian "heaven," but rather "initiating." The reason for this is that heaven, according to the ancient sage, refers to celestial bodies or the divine deity known as the Heavenly Elderly Father. From studying the *I Ching* or mythology one can gain an understanding of the relationships between heaven and earth and apply this philosophical instruction to life.

One also must understand the strength of receptivity, the strength of the earth. The earth is represented in myth and symbolism in virtually every corner of the globe. The Greeks and Romans named earth *Gaia* or *Ge*—the Latin root of such English words as "geology" and "geography." Earth was the offspring of Chaos and was a mother-goddess. She gave birth to the sky, Uranus, who later became her husband. It is interesting to see the common threads among the stories told in ancient cultures. Heaven and earth are in perpetual relationship: intertwined, utterly interdependent, and inseparable.

SACRED GEOLOGY

The Chinese character Qian is the name of the first hexagram in the I Ching

Preserved within sacred texts are not just stories of our creation, but also practical knowledge we need in order to bridge the spiritual and material worlds. Just as early mythological accounts tell of times of endless mud from which a deity refined the solid earth, modern geologists verify a kind of sedimentary genesis.

We are never far removed from this genesis, according to Gregg Braden in his book, *The God Code*. Braden shows us how the human body is literally composed of earthly elements: "The Creator asked his angels to 'go and fetch me dust from the four corners of the Earth, and I will create man therewith'." [2]

According to the Book of Genesis, a form was molded from the finest particles of earth to embody an image of the Creator: "By His word, He formed a person [*adam*] from the dust of the ground [*adamah*] and breathed into his nostrils the breath of life." In Hebrew, the word for man is "Adam" (*ADM*), which is derived from the root word *adamah*. Interestingly, *adamah* is also the Hebrew word for "land" or "ground," indicating a direct and personal relationship between Adam and the earth. In deriving the word Adam from *adamah,* the ancients emphasize that the first human was formed from the elements of the earth. A literal translation would state that Adam is a person, a man, "of the ground." It follows that Adam's mate, a feminine archetype for the original woman, is named Eve, which is a word with shared roots for "heaven" and "ether."

The relationship between humankind and the earth is also widely acknowledged today in our funeral services. We say that a life's journey is a circle, with-

The Creation, *from the Luther Bible, c.1530 (woodcut). The Bridgeman Art Library*

Marc Chagall, **The Creation of Man,** *1956-58 (oil on canvas).*
Musée Marc Chagall, Nice, France. The Bridgeman Art Library

out beginning and without end, yet transformative throughout as we pass from "ashes to ashes and dust to dust." There is much truth in this saying, for the human body is composed of natural elements.

Together, initiating heaven energy and yielding earth energy comprise a complete cosmos out of which life is brought into being and into which it returns. The relationship of active and passive principles is present within us at all times in the apparent duality of our sensory, physical experience of life—as well as in our more subtle spiritual experiences: body and soul.

Centering Practice: The Tree Pose

1. Begin by bringing hands together in prayer position.
2. Shift weight to your left foot. Inhale and lift the right foot and place above the knee inside the thigh. *Do not place your foot directly on the knee joint.* (Alternate position: Right foot rests inside left ankle or mid-calf.)

LEFT: **Step 1**

RIGHT: **Step 2**

3. Take a few breaths to center yourself. Imagine that your left foot is a root anchoring you in the ground. Return your hands to the prayer position.

4. Express your own personal tree. This can take various forms. Some trees sway with the wind, other stand tall and proud, other open themselves up to the sun. Be creative, but also mindful of your groundedness. Remain comfortably receptive to upward rising energy. Once you stabilize your balance you can go through the different positions in a kind of moving meditation.

ABOVE (L-R): **Step 4**

5. Return to the original position, bringing hands together in front of your heart and your foot back to the ground. As you exhale forward fold at the waist. You can bend your knees or keep them straight. You may wish to remain in this position for five breaths, letting go of tension in your upper back and neck. Let the weight of your head naturally stretch your neck.

6. Relaxed and recharged, return slowly to the upright position.

7. Repeat the sequence standing on your right foot.

Step 5

CHAPTER FOUR

The Four Pillars of Health

He that eateth well, drinketh well.
He that drinketh well, sleepeth well.
He that sleepeth well, sinneth not.
He that sinneth not, goeth straight
From Purgatory to Paradise.
—William Lithgow, rare adventures

TRADITIONAL MEDICINE tells us that our health can be likened to a table: it stands only with four pillars of equal stability. The four pillars of health are as follows:

FOOD

EXERCISE

SLEEP

PLEASURE

This approach is about lifestyle balance, or the process of balancing momentary and enduring satisfactions. It is recommended that we find vital, creative, nourishing, and stimulating ingredients to fill our lives. It's interesting that behavioral approaches to weight loss, depression, addictions, and creativity often mention the same ideas: eat a balanced diet; engage in a variety of activities; get enough rest; don't live passively; don't dwell on things that upset you; reconnect with your higher purpose; and so on.

Each of the four pillars is a category of choices that are within our control. However, in order to balance our lifestyle effectively we need to approach it as a process, not as a single event.

FOUR PILLARS
LIFE BALANCE PROGRAM:
28 DAYS TO VITALITY

Ancient healers taught a two-part approach to life, healing, and achieving balance in all relationships. In the imagistic, dualistic theory of these healing traditions, all manifestations reflect two opposing and complementary energies. Perpetually expanding and contracting, initiating and responding, these two fundamental energies are represented in pairings, or dichotomies, with such names as heaven/earth, masculine/feminine, receptive/initiating.

We can apply the principle of these paired correspondences to modify our lifestyle in a variety of ways over the course of four weeks. Each week, make one modification to each of the four pillars of health in two steps. These two steps are the practical application of your inner paired forces of heaven/earth, masculine/feminine, and receptive/initiating.

Step one is reduction. This is the "earth" phase of your change, during which you are yielding and softening. The earth principle within us is often referred to as soft, yielding, and receptive. Much like a "mother" who guides us to live as she lives—gently yet powerfully, with resilience and strength—within each

of us resides such innate yielding strength. The ability to give way is to ebb and flow without rigidity, to move with, rather than against. This power, when combined with the passion of the active principle, achieves change through "effortless effort"; through "non-doing" rather than doing. It leads to reduced consumption and diminished attachment.

Step two is "active replacement" or "reimplementation." This is the "heaven" phase of your program, and represents the active principle. The energy of heaven, in the form of ideas, passions, or action, must have something to act upon and inspire into being. It needs a matrix to work through, to channel itself into manifestation. Step two is our capacity for action. This may be actualized in a vibrant exercise program; in shopping for, cooking, and eating nutritious foods; or in changing one's thought patterns from negative to positive.

Consider your own life and the changes that you plan to make. It is helpful to recognize that each person has inherent strengths as well as inherent weaknesses. In other words, you may have three very stable pillars and one that is relatively underdeveloped. This is natural. It is therefore advised that you begin with your strengths, stabilizing your energy first before proceeding to change your weakest area.

Soul-Centered Goal Planning

The problem with many ancient healing models is that they seem vague, full of expressions of perfection or ideals rather than clear plans of action. Soul-centered lifestyle goals are based on the truth of who we are. They represent both the initiative of heaven and the endurance of earth and as such help us see this passage through to completion. Soul-centered lifestyle goals are self-directed.

What advantages do soul-centered goals have for rebalancing our lives? They provide inner direction as well as structure. They direct our attention to solutions while diffusing negative focus.

A four-week program allows for the structure needed to measure growth. It can be repeated, revised, improved upon, accelerated, or discontinued at the end of the four weeks. Each person's goals are unique to his or her own soul. When we create our own plan in this way, we are more likely to be successful than if someone else creates a plan for us. This approach also works because it is gentle and forgiving, rather than austere or punitive. Ancient healing traditions do not share the tendency of modern westerners to "medicalize" (diagnose or label) a condition with words, which can fix a negative pattern more deeply in the mind.

Achieving soul-centered goals requires a process of conscious planning, not just thinking about an earnest desire. Planning is best done in a calm atmosphere, and it can be done quite effectively in ten minutes a day.

Start simply and build your awareness and goals.

Establish and review your short-term and long-term goals.

Plan your activities with those goals in mind.

A review of where we are—emotionally, personally, physically, spiritually—is a good way to begin a plan for where we want to be. Prepare for the process about one week in advance by getting a journal. On the top of four separate pages, write the words:

F O O D

S L E E P

E X E R C I S E

P L E A S U R E

BALANCING OUR FOOD

ON THE FOOD PAGE. Keep track of your daily intake of food groups. Note whether you cooked at home or ate out; also record the time of day you ate each meal. Jot down any recurring moods, physical symptoms, or sensitivities.

Of the four elements in nature, food correlates to the earth element so it may likely be the most important change to address. In the imagery of traditional healing, earth is said to provide cohesion, substance, stamina, and physical strength. If we expand the category of food to embody cellular nourishment of all sorts, we may more fully appreciate each meal as an aspect of conscious creation.

Likewise, proper food combining and knowledge of seasonal adaptations in diet may make the difference between food as fuel and food as poison. Instinctively, we know it is not intelligent to eat the same thing every day of the year. Yet many of us become lulled into a certain monotony at mealtime, day after day.

Healthy eating starts with cooking. Do you cook at home often? Your kitchen is the heart of your home. When it lies stagnant, all areas of your life will suffer. The more you cook at home, the happier and healthier you will be. If you can't cook, be sure to ignite the burners on your stove at least once a day to generate warmth and vitality.

Ask yourself which foods and beverages you are now consuming daily that may be out of harmony with your body or the current season. If you eat too many sweets, reduce the daily quantity that you are currently indulging in by one fourth the first week. The second week, subtract the same amount, and so on, until by the end of the fourth week this food is gone from your diet. At the same time, add to your diet a healthy complement. For example, as you reduce processed sweets, you may choose to increase fresh fruits and vegetables. So, during Week 1 add one fourth more fruits and vegetables to your diet; by the end of the fourth week, your diet will have been positively modified. This approach is intentionally intuition-based, without fussy measurements and nutritional analysis.

> *Step one focuses on the reduction of habitual eating and indulgence.*
>
> *Step two focuses on the introduction of a nourishing alternative.*

BALANCING OUR SLEEP

ON THE SLEEP PAGE. Keep track of your daily sleep schedule. Note whether you have awakened refreshed or rushed, and jot down any difficulties sleeping, sleep aids taken, or remarkable dream states.

"Even sleepers are workers and collaborators in what goes on in the universe"
—HERACLITUS

For the Australian aborigine "the dreamtime" signifies connectedness with ancestors and the earth

54

The second category, sleep, is vital for our health. In the quaternity of the natural elements, sleep and dreams correlate to the water element. It is known that sleep is crucial to a strong immune system. Studies have found that adults require seven to eight hours of sleep every day. Chronic sleep deprivation, with only five or six hours each day, can have a negative impact on immunity.

According to the Australian Aborigines, when a person "loses his dreaming, he is lost." In deep sleep and certain meditative states, human brain waves can be measured at between 8 and 13 hertz. Coincidentally, the earth oscillates at around 10 hertz. So in our deepest mystery of consciousness, that is, during deep sleep, we enter into synchrony with the earth.

It is in sleep that we may best process excess mental and visual impressions, reviewing the emotional content of our lives without the interference of cognitive analysis. When faced with a problem, sometimes we can "sleep on it," a way of allowing the creative potential of our unconscious mind to work on an issue.

Sleep deprivation and even mild sleep interruption play a role in certain medical conditions such as fibromyalgia, or chronic muscle pain and fatigue. Sleep studies done with athletic, fit males in their early twenties have shown that in as little as three weeks' time regular sleep interruption may actually induce fibromyalgia, nervous system disorders, joint pain, headaches, and depression.

How is your sleep? Do you awaken feeling energized?

FOR BETTER DREAMS. According to Feng Shui, you can implement water cures for your bedroom to increase dreams. Low lighting and plenty of plump pillows and plush fabrics are powerful treatments to deepen lucid dreaming. Be sure to keep the television out of your bedroom, or you'll spend more time watching movies than creating your own. Soft watercolors or photos of seascapes in the bedroom will lend a satisfying sweetness to your sleep life.

IF YOU SUFFER CHRONIC STRESS AND FATIGUE. Go to bed ten minutes earlier each night during the first week. During Weeks 2, 3 and 4, set your alarm clock for ten minutes earlier every morning and then claim that "extra" time and energy as your own. After four weeks, you will be getting to bed earlier and getting up earlier, with more quiet time to yourself.

"The net of sleep catches fish"
—GREEK PROVERB

Step one focuses on the reduction of fatigue and on getting more rest.

Step two focuses on the implementation of a nourishing alternative: more quiet time alone in the morning when you have more energy.

BALANCING OUR EXERCISE

ON THE EXERCISE PAGE. Keep track of your daily exercise, activities, and recreational outings. Also jot down any stimulants or sedatives including caffeine, beer, wine, herbs, and vitamins or supplements taken daily.

From the four-element perspective, exercise is the expression of fire. This is not surprising when you consider that it raises metabolism, or the burning of

Sleep is nature's most effective restorative

fuel for energy. The category of exercise reaches beyond uninspiring repetitive activity. The underlying benefit of exercise is movement, whose main purpose is cleansing. Although the human body is designed as a self-renewing organism, it relies upon regular internal purification. We all have the potential to become congested to varying degrees. In this regard, the natural law of similars applies: "like attracts like." Inactivity attracts aimlessness, which fosters passivity, which leads to more inertia.

This cycle may begin in the mind. In this instance just getting up and doing something that occupies your mind can be an important part of enacting change—even if you don't feel like it at the moment. Let your body lead by engaging in aerobic exercises, and your mind can follow. Or, inactivity can be felt primarily in the body. In this case let your mind lead your body, as with Pilates or Yoga methods. Either way, movement is key to clearing away built-up toxic byproducts of diet, metabolism, and environmental pollutants. Exercise stimulates circulation and produces heat, which in turn promotes sweating and activates elimination.

Are you getting enough exercise and movement every day? If not, try this:

If you are currently not exercising at all, during the first week get down on the floor in the morning and stretch for five minutes. For the second week, continue with your stretching and add ten minutes every other day of brisk exercise such as jogging around your neighborhood, cycling the block, bouncing in place, or dancing to music that you really love. For the third week, maintain the stretching and aerobic exercises, but increase the aerobic movement time by five minutes. For the fourth week, increase the workout time and intensity, or try walking during your lunch break in addition to your exercises. After four weeks, you will feel much more energized and fit.

Step one focuses on the reduction of lethargy, sluggishness, and inertia by the introduction of stretching.

Step two focuses on implementation of a stimulating alternative such as aerobics.

BALANCING OUR PLEASURE

ON THE PLEASURE PAGE. Keep track of your daily moods, dreams, issues, feelings, and attitudes. This journaling process is not meant to be burdensome and time-consuming; rather, it is a way to become true to yourself and aware of ingrained patterns. For example, you may not even be aware that you suffer fatigue at the same time each day, or that you crave a certain food or drink in response to a person or responsibility in your life. Simply record any emerging patterns daily at bedtime and in the morning.

This pillar is more spiritual than physical, and as such it represents the element air in our experience. According to medieval astrologers the air element is centered in the lungs and emotional heart center. This is the place in our physical body that registers joy and grief through relationship with the world. Including pleasure in daily life is a health category that modern Western medicine would hardly consider a "minimum daily requirement," but it may give the

most meaning to one's life. In the original teachings from Asia, this category translated as the cultivation of all five pathways of cognition: sight, smell, hearing, taste, and touch—importantly, not for their own sake, but instead as offerings of gratitude to the divine.

Put simply: when we appreciate the light upon this earth, when we are grateful for the majesty of a mountain range, when we tend a garden or draw artistic inspiration from the force of a winter storm or hurricane, we merge our personal experience, for a moment at least, with consciousness of unity in all things.

We should engage in pleasurable, enjoyable acts that are in keeping with our true character; this way they are beneficial rather than mere indulgences. Are you appreciating the beauty around you as fully as possibly? Do you feel gratitude for your share of the simple pleasures in life?

If you are having trouble with this pillar, answer one question: What are the things you do on a day-to-day basis that make you feel comfortable, or that give you at least some sense of well-being? Write them down. It is sometimes necessary to consciously look for the small, uneventful, happy moments that are occurring all the time; we can blind ourselves to them when we are stressed, anxious, or depressed. Now here's an idea: try to do at least some of those things every day. Your task in this area of life is to perpetually strengthen yourself, as commentary from the *I Ching* prescribes, "as thunder and wind strengthen each other." This is certainly an internal change. For instance, if you see something good in another, imitate it; and when you see something inferior in your own attitude, try to eliminate it.

> *Step one focuses on the reduction of dullness and negativity by opening the eyes of the heart.*

> *Step two focuses on implementation of a stimulating alternative such as increased appreciation for beauty.*

The purpose of establishing goals is to become clear-minded and effective at achieving what we want, rather than to simply be busy. It is easy to be caught up in the activity trap and stay quite busy while accomplishing very little. Set your goals with the end in mind: look at what you want based on your values, and then set a daily path for that goal. In four weeks' time look back and see what you have accomplished. Rather than dwelling at the time of reappraisal on what you haven't accomplished, ask these questions without judging yourself or labeling yourself a success or failure:

1. *What worked?*

2. *What else did you accomplish? What were the unintended consequences?*

3. *Did your goals change? Is it time to make some new goals?*

4. *Are you still on track toward your long-term objectives?*

ANCIENT ENERGY TIP

IF YOUR FOCUS IS ON REDUCING—such as weight loss, breaking a habit, ending a relationship, eliminating negative thinking—the best time to start this program is on the Full Moon.

TO FOCUS ON INCREASING—such as establishing and sticking to a financial budget, building muscular strength, starting a creative project, or gaining more energy in general—the best time to start this program is on the New (or Dark) Moon.

ANOTHER LIFE-HEALING PRACTICE

This is a more difficult practice to put into action. The emphasis is on the word "practice," as you will never be finished with this one!

> *It is very beneficial to keep a consciousness of simplicity in life whenever possible.*

Whose life does not have room for improvement here? Remember the analogy of the stream to our health? When earth and water are in healthy relationship, a stream flows. On the other hand, when they are out of balance, we get mud.

If you find you are in a muddled state of mind regarding a relationship, a career, or in general, try to reduce the excessive amount of activity you are engaged in at any one time. Do only what you are doing, and be only where you are. There is a joke shared among Buddhists about this very difficult challenge:

One day, three Buddhist monks met on a mountain pass. The first one proceeded to brag about his teacher and how accomplished he was. He enumerated many feats of amazing complexity that the teacher had performed, such as walking on water and sleeping on a bed of nails.

The second monk went on to outdo the first monk, praising his own spiritual teacher by telling of his mastery of his body. His teacher could breathe so efficiently that he took only one breath per day, inhaling at sunrise and exhaling at sunset.

Now the third monk was silent, listening. Finally, when asked about his own teacher, he replied, "My teacher is very powerful. He eats when he eats, walks when he walks, and sits when he sits."

Kawanabe Kyosai, Daruma

(ink on paper)
© Indianapolis Museum of Art, USA / Mr and Mrs Richard Crane Fund/ The Bridgeman Art Library.

Daruma, also known as Bodhidharma, is considered to be the founder of Zen Buddhism

MEDICINE FROM THE BEGINNING OF TIME: FROM CAVE DWELLERS TO AYURVEDA TO WESTERN MEDICINE

"Every ingredient in the cosmos has a healing effect—every plant, flower, stone, leaf, bark, aroma... We just need to learn how to use them properly."

—DR. NAINA MARBALLI, BSAM, DAC
DIRECTOR OF AYURVEDA'S BEAUTY CARE CENTER, NEW YORK CITY

USING STONES WITH oils, flowers, herbs, and other elements of the earth as a way to facilitate our innate healing potential is as old as humanity. Paleoarcheologists have uncovered evidence showing that warm earth, clay, and stones were used, probably instinctively, to treat a wide range of injuries and diseases from the very beginning of human development.

The earliest human-related population on earth, known as "hominids," evolved as primates about 4.5 million years ago. While there are no data to indicate that organized medicine or healing systems existed at that time, primitive illustrations have been found in carvings and cave paintings indicating that stones, sometimes wrapped with herbs, were heated in the sun and then applied to the body.

Stones used in massage therapy today are sourced from some of the oldest rock formations on the planet, dating back 450 million and 600 million years. Perhaps the same stones we are discovering today were used by our ancient forebears in their own healing rituals!

OPPOSITE: **Karl Bodmer,** Medicine Man of the Mandan Tribe in the Costume of the Dog Dance, *1834 (color litho). Private Collection/ Peter Newark American Pictures/ The Bridgeman Art Library*

Vaidya Dhanvantari, Supreme Saint of Ayurveda Medicine.

©Private Collection/ Dinodia/ The Bridgeman Art Library

The oldest known texts on healing, and the system known today as Ayurveda, are thought to be around five thousand years old. The word *Ayurveda* may be translated as "the lore of life," "the science of life," or "the art of self healing." Ancient Indian sages compiled their medical material from many sources. The texts that set down their understanding of the healing process as well as their vision of the world and the cosmos are known as the *Vedas*. *Veda* is a Sanskrit root word for "life," and is closely related to the Latin root word for life, *vita*.

Ayurvedic medicine began as a manual of magic. After its incantational medicine had evolved into empirical medicine, the most important of all Ayurvedic texts appeared. The *Charaka Samhita* dates from between the eighth and eleventh centuries BC.

Students of Ayurveda studied practical arts such as cookery; collection and preparation of herbs; and purification and preparation of the stone, gems, and crystals used in mineral medicines. One word for stone in Sanskrit is "*shila*", and reference to its therapeutic use is found in many sources. For instance, applications still being used today by naturopaths and Ayurvedic practitioners ae compounds made from rocks.

High in the Himalayan Mountains, a thick rich paste can be found oozing out from the rocks in the towering cliffs. It is called *shilajit*. It is a form of mineral that drips from the cracks of the rocks during hot weather and is composed of plant matter from millennia past. The bio-transformed plant matter is extruded from the rocks by geothermal pressures. It is collected in raw form for further purification. *Shilajit* is believed to increase the energy that is depleted by stress and anxiety.

Another tradition of earth medicine from India that is still in practice today is the ingestion of specially prepared ashes from ground gemstones such as emeralds, diamonds and rubies.

By comparison, the precise origins of traditional Chinese medicine are obscure. Descriptions of early medical practices in China are found in the *The Yellow*

Emperor's Inner Classic, written some time between the third and fifth centuries BC. Included is a summation of the different medical approaches and practices found at that time in China. Subsequent works laid the groundwork for the system that has come down to us today.

Contained within these books are the therapeutic modalities of moxabustion (heat therapy), acupuncture, massage, remedial exercise, and the use of plant and mineral medicines. Moxabustion involves the application of burning herbs—and in some instances heated stones—directly to the skin at specific points along the surface of the body. It is a practice that is now being redefined in massage; some massage practitioners integrate warm stones into meridian-based therapies.

Beginning around the eighth century BC, the Iron Age in China, the properties of lodestone (i.e. magnetic rock) were discovered. During this period, bone needles used in acupuncture were replaced by magnetic stone needles.

Historically, each region of the world has cultivated a thorough appreciation for the earth and its healing clays and healing stones. The Essenes, famed authors of the Dead Sea Scrolls, the Australian Aborigines, and Mexican and South American Indian cultures all recognized their benefits. Bentonite and other types of healing clay such as illite have been used by indigenous cultures since before recorded history. Although mankind's use of this living crystal has spanned the globe, very little information has been preserved regarding specific methodologies. However, this much is known: the greatest lost cultures of ancient civilization gave healing clays a position of major importance in ceremonial usage.

Natives of North America utilized a wide variety of clays for healing, physical purification and the purification of food; and for spiritual ceremonies. Quality clay, highly prized for trade with other tribes, formed a significant part of their cultures. It was used in sweat lodge ceremonies and taken with food to prevent stomach illness. Clay dyed with berries was used as facial paint by tribal warriors.

The Egyptians used clay extensively in their spiritual culture. High quality clay was the prime ingredient in their unmatched embalming process, helping to perfectly preserve mummified bodies for thousands of years. It is safe to assume that they used clay for other purposes as well, yet much of what we know of this ancient culture is built from incomplete data and is therefore speculative.

CHAPTER SIX

SELF WORTH, SELF EARTH: TAPPING INTO YOUR INNER VEIN OF GOLD

"To live content with small means; to seek elegance rather than luxury, and refinement rather than fashion; to be worthy, not respectable, and wealthy, not rich; to study hard, think quietly, talk gently, act frankly; to listen to stars and birds, to babes and sages, with open heart; to bear all cheerfully, do all bravely, await occasions, hurry never. In a word, to let the spiritual, unbidden and unconscious, grow up through the common. This is to be my symphony."

— WILLIAM HENRY CHANNING

WHAT IS OUR relationship with money and material abundance? To find the answer to this question, we may ask not how much do money do we have, but, rather, how much energy do we express, channel, and share? For, wealth is the circulation of energy here on earth. Is your work an expression of loving service to the world, or, is it merely an obligation to be endured? In this chapter we will explore the true meaning of wealth, our spiritual value systems, and the lessons we may take from our life experience.

To prosper means to grow spiritually along all lines. One of the basic tenets of spirituality and abundance is the importance of participating in a circle of giving and receiving. Acts of material generosity are the path to material prosperity. On the other hand, practices which infuse us with more vital energy are believed to make us more attractive and magnetic. These values may guide us in making our everyday exchanges more sacred. Here is an affirmation which

OPPOSITE: **The Hindu God Ganesha is the remover of obstacles. One looks to him for success in every new enterprise.**

67

"It ascends from the earth to the heaven and again it descends to the earth and receives the force of things superior and inferior."

—FROM THE EMERALD TABLET OF HERMES TRISMIGISTUS

may be used as a meditation for adjusting your perspective in relation to the flow of wealth in your life:

At the center of my being

is peace.

In this stillness, I feel the strength and the support of the earth and the creative universal force.

At the center of my being,

I am a channel for this creative universal force here on earth.

I am always guided to my perfect service and expression in life.

As a channel for the earth's creative universal force

I am compensated in wonderful ways.

All of my exchanges are fair exchanges. For this I am grateful.

I see the creative universal force personified in all people everywhere on this earth. Because of this knowledge, I am filled with joy and harmony.

I know that as I invite this river of peace to flow through my being, the way out of struggle is revealed to me. All that I need to fully express and serve on this earth are irresistibly attracted to me by the universal laws of attraction. For this I am grateful.

The meaning of life, or, a life of meaning, has been a perennial pursuit in the history of humanity. However, the gap between material reality and our ideal, reflects the essential battle between matter and spirit. In the light of ancient spiritual traditions, a four-tiered value system has been constructed which traces the ladder of spiritual development, starting with satisfactions of the lower impulses and physical needs, progressing through intermediate steps which lead to still higher levels of consciousness, eventually providing liberation from the lower impulses and needs and the full experience of spiritual peace.

Even the word "value" was originally used to mean "worth", mainly in political economy. Over time, the meaning of "value" has broadened and is used in a wider sense to connote worth, intrinsic goodness, desirability, usefulness, etc. In its even wider sense, however, value covers the entire field of human life. All kinds of rightness—virtue, morality, religion, truth, law, custom, arts, science, and talent, health, family, friendship, and beauty—are among our current values.

Value appreciation may differ from person to person and from culture to culture. Cultural conditions are very closely related to the value system, although there are some universal values. Controversy will always remain over the question of whether something is valuable because it is desired, or, is desired because it is valuable.

In order to understand the principles of prosperity it is essential to look at the roots of our value system both theoretically and practically. Theoretical considerations include the nature of spirituality, deities, souls and their relationship with this world; practical considerations are centered on the actuality of our daily experiences.

The idea of a fundamental cosmic order lies at the root of ancient value systems. This order is observed throughout the universe. In ancient Sanskrit, the word representing this order is "*rta*", and is defined as being universal, controlling, and encompassing gods, men, and nature. It is because of *rta* that the creation is a cosmos, and not a chaos.

The word "*rta*" is related through "*ar*" to "*harmos*" (Greek) and "*ars*" (Latin), forming the sources of words such as harmony and art. The word conveys the experience of a finely tuned Universe. All of heaven and earth belong to *rta*.

"*Rta*" has been spelled out for us in Sanskrit as a word "*artha*", which can also be translated as earth, wealth, or end (as in goal). Sanskrit is full of subtlety and layers, and for each word there are numerous applications. In this case, then, "*artha*" refers to wealth in terms of tangible as well as intangible measures. For example, your "wealth" includes, in addition to your money, property, and hard assets, qualities such as talents, skills, abilities, experience, and also what is dear to you, such as your family, spouse, garden, and business.

One of the Vedic texts, the *Atharva Veda*, teaches that life is based on perpetual compromise between desires and duties. The desire to create is said to be the first seed of the mind, a dictum that acknowledges that desire is a fact of human experience.

There are prayers for wealth and material prosperity, acquisition and preservation of property, as well as rules for the promotion of welfare,

"The creation and attainment of artha, wealth, is one of the four goals of human life."
—RIG VEDA

prescribed in the Vedas. These prayers indicate that the early Vedic civilization paid attention to the material life and was aware of practical needs. Freedom from debt is an object of desire in some ancient Vedic hymns.

"May we be free in this world and that yonder, in the third world may we be unindebted. May we, debt-free, abide in all the pathways, in the worlds which Gods and Fathers visit."
(ATHARVA VEDA 6.117.3)

Man's life itself is viewed as a debt to God, mankind, and the earth, and it was believed that it is man's duty to repay these debts. The *Taittreya Brahmana* speaks of these debts as being fourfold in nature. We are counseled to serve, in the following order: God, family, nation (or community), and (sacred) science.

This concept of life and this ancient value system is therefore ethically oriented, recognizing that the individual has certain obligations. By such actions as service, caring for family and animals, contributing to our community and studying science, we become free of our debts. Put another way, by sharing our wealth with others, through hospitality and material generosity, we become free of our debts to society and to the earth. It is our duty to do these things.

In order to enjoy greater prosperity and material wealth, it was said that one should seek it by the path of *rta*, or *dharma*. "*Dharma*" is more commonly used than "*rta*", but it signifies a similar concept. It is also used to describe righteousness, sustained duty, upholding the laws of the universe, religious merit, custom. In some contexts it is used to reflect the sum total of social, religious, and moral values.

Although this may sound lofty and out of reach for us today, these ancient teachings show us ways to embrace earthly life and worldly wealth as good. We can see that earth was often glorified as an object of profound respect and love, and that wealth is both a material and a spiritual value. This explains the basis of natural healing practices aimed at promoting unimpaired longevity, supporting a body with all the senses fully engaged.

Numerous rites for material prosperity clearly show that economic value was greatly appreciated. An active, engaged life is also praised.

"The gods befriend none but one who has toiled."
(RIG VEDA 4.33.11)

Lassitude hampers a person's prosperity.

> *"Manifest is the prosperity of him who is weary. His body grows and is fruitful. All his sins disappear, slain by the toil of his journeying."* (AITAREYA BRAHMANA)

> *"The fortune of him who sitteth also sitteth, But that of him who standeth erect is upright, that of him that reclineth lieth down. The fortune of him that moveth shall move indeed."* (AITAREYA BRAHMANA)

So we see that pursuit of desires, achieving goals, and striving for a more effective existence is timeless.

Meditation on Earth's Abundance and Wealth

Have a pad of paper and pen handy for this exercise.

Sit or lie comfortably. Unplug the phone and create a space that will not be interrupted for ten to fifteen minutes.

Without effort or trying to change the way you naturally breathe, inhale and exhale fully and deeply, in and out through your nose. Bring your breath all the way down to the abdomen and into your back.

There is no need to pull the air in forcefully, nor is there any benefit to be gained from pushing the air out strongly. Try to keep a silent breath, rather than a noisy stream of air. With a softened inner gaze, try to observe, or, if you are a more kinesthetic type of person, see if you are able to sense, any areas in your body that feel dense or tight, where the breath does not so easily stretch the skin from the inside out. Don't engage in judgments. Simply witness the movements of your mind. Focusing on the sensations that arise as you breathe bridges the chasm separating body and mind, allowing you to become fully present in your body, and more aware of the messages you may be holding for yourself.

Continue to breathe fully and deeply. Match the length of the exhale to the inhale, gradually lengthening them and slowing your complete breathing rhythm.

Now, for the next few minutes, contemplate the Earth as an "all-sustaining, treasure-bearing resting place." Contemplate the nature of money and wealth, and what these words mean to you, and only to you, not to your culture or society or your family. Notice what feelings and sensations may arise. Especially observe any tightness of breath or shortness of inhalation. Repeat the question to yourself:

"What is the nature of money and wealth in my life?"

Stay connected with your breath during the practice, and you may receive some insights related to your attitudes or financial condition. Notice any repetitive thoughts, such as those having to do with lack, limitation, struggle, or desire. Again, don't judge these thoughts. Just witness them.

When you are complete with this meditation, open your eyes, and begin the writing portion of the practice. Write at the top of the page: "Money" (or "Wealth" or "Vitality") is pure energy in circulation."

Life offers us many choices and ways to exchange our energy with others to make it grow more. If we view money and wealth as an exchange of pure energy with two aspects, giving and receiving, we will see that if we enjoy the gifts of the earth and our life without offering something in return, we dissipate our energy, and our (inner) wealth grows very little.

Finish your exercise now by listing three actions you will take to give and receive the full blessings of the earth.

According to the Vedic laws of giving and receiving, each of us comes into life with four sacred pathways in the circle of sharing: a promise, a gift, a passion, and a deep desire.

YOUR PROMISE is that which you came to life to master. Your soul has lessons to learn, debts and duties to fulfill, experiences to go through. When we resist our promise, our lessons, and our duties, we feel stressed and tense, and our lives will feel as though they lack meaning. If we are open to these experiences as part of an agreement made at the soul level, we may become more peaceful within. It is from this place that we serve God.

YOUR GIFT is what you have to offer. The gift consists of innate strengths and talents, skills mastered perhaps in previous lifetimes or assets that come easily to you in this one. The gift is the seed of your self actualization. These are special things that you, and only you, can do. The gift is how you serve the study of science and the development of ideas for the benefit of humanity.

YOUR PASSION represents those things that you pursue for freedom, liberty, joy, pleasure, and happiness. These worldly values make life worth living. By protecting your passion you serve your community, your nation and your ancestors.

YOUR HEARTFELT DESIRE is the value that you hold most dear and is often the thing you want most to experience in life. You may want love, acceptance, compassion, health, wellbeing, support, or security. Becoming aware of your deepest heartfelt desire is one way you may serve your family, animals, plants, the earth itself, and your ancestors.

The cornucopia (horn of plenty) symbolizes the abundant harvest.

CHAPTER SEVEN

SACRED SITES AND HOLY LANDS

EVERY CIVILIZATION since the beginning of recorded history has recognized that certain regions of the earth are associated with "divine" influences. It is believed that subtle magnetic forces emanate from holy sites, drawing people from far away for healing, renewal, and communion with the spirit realm. "Holy" lands have had a tremendous cultural impact worldwide; beliefs associated with such lands have left their imprint, influencing the course of our modern-day civilization.

Are the spiritual traditions associated with sacred lands purely cultural practices, or is there a basis for these traditions in a tangible and physical reality? Is there something scientifically unique about the lands honored by the peoples of the world?

Locations in nature that are prized by indigenous cultures, upon careful examination, often reveal rare or distinctive elements that are conducive to human development and healing.

Sacred lands often have one of the following characteristics:

1. *A history of near-surface volcanic activity;*

2. *A highly specialized water and or mineral source; glacial, inter-mountain or ground-to-surface river sources; filtration mineral hot, or warm, springs;*

3. *Areas with rare and highly specialized ecosystems;*

4. *Subtle anomalies associated with electromagnetic energy fields generating sonic wave forms, possibly as the result of geothermal activity or an unusually high concentration of monoatomic elements in the environment.*

Forecourt of temple in Chichen Itza

Here we will explore some of the better-known sites:

1. **BRITISH ISLES:** *Stonehenge*

2. **ARCTIC:** *Streams of the Sami*

3. **INDIA:** *The Ganges River*

4. **JAPAN:** *Mount Fuji*

5. **CENTRAL AMERICA:** *Tikal, Chichen Itza, and the Mirador*

6. **AFRICA:** *Mount Kenya*

7. **USA:** *Devils Tower, Wyoming; Wolf River, Wisconsin; Weatherman Draw, Montana; Petroglyph National Monument, New Mexico; Mauna Kea, Hawaii*

STONEHENGE   Stone circles are found primarily within the British Isles. There are about a thousand known sites. In the Neolithic Age some five thousand years ago, the people of the British Isles began constructing circular spaces marked by boundaries of purposefully-erected stones. They also created rings of earth, called *henges*. Their lives were wholly dependent on the forces of the earth and nature, and their belief system certainly reflected that connectedness. Stones were often aligned with the rising or setting of the sun or moon at certain times of the year, indicating concepts of the cycle of life and by extension, fertility.

Circles ranged in size from about ten to more than one thousand feet in diameter. The transportation, arrangement, and erection of such massive stones were truly engineering feats. Some of the finest megalithic rings were erected in the centuries around 2400 BC, and prehistoric people continued to build stone circles until about 1500 BC, during the Bronze Age.

Archaeologists, geologists and mathematicians have generated innumerable speculations about the origin and purpose of the stone circles. Some of the more commonly proposed scenarios include temples, courts of justice, cemeteries, calendars, and celestial observatories. The structures were integrally connected to the belief system of the prehistoric people who built them.

Stonehenge in early morning

The Roman invasion of the first century brought recorded history to the British Isles, but nothing was written about the stone circles. It is known that as the ever-growing Christian church attempted to stamp out pagan practice, it issued edicts condemning beliefs connected to natural objects, including stones. In at least one area it ordered that churches should be built wherever standing stones were found. Such evidence supports the theory that the megalithic rings continued to be used, or at least venerated; their power continued to be recognized, generating folk tales and superstitions that were passed down through generations.

SAMI SACRED STREAMS. The Sami are one of Europe's oldest ethnic groups. Since prehistoric times they have lived in the region best known as Lapland, now called Sapmi or Samiland. Today they are formally recognized as "Sami" (also spelled in English as Saami or Sámi)—which means "the people"—rather than "Laplander," a derogatory term imposed by colonial powers. The Sami practice a shamanistic spirituality rooted in a respectful, harmonious relationship with nature. The land itself is sacred and is also marked with specific holy sites. *Sieidit* (stones in natural or human-built formations), *álda* and *sáivu* (sacred hills),

Arctic lakes and streams

springs, caves, and other natural formations serve as altars where prayers and offerings are made. Through a type of sing-song chant called the *joik*, Sami convey legends and express their spirituality. *Noiade* are individuals who communicate with the spirits and intercede on behalf of the community. The *suttesaja*, (places of healing in nature) which means "stream that doesn't freeze over," are now protected by the Finnish National Board of Antiquities.

THE SACRED RIVER GANGES Winding 1,560 miles across northern India, from the Himalaya Mountains to the Indian Ocean, the Ganges River is not a sacred place: it is a sacred entity. Known as *Ganga Ma*—Mother Ganges—the river is revered as a goddess whose purity cleanses the sins of the faithful and aids the dead on their path toward heaven. According to Hindu mythology, the Ganges was once a river of heaven that flowed across the sky. Long ago, she agreed to fall to earth to aid a king named Bhagiratha, whose ancestors had been burned to ash by the angry gaze of an ascetic they had disturbed during meditation. Only the purifying waters of Ganges flowing over the ashes could free them from the earth and raise them up to live in peace in heaven.

So that the earth would not be shattered by the impact of her descent, Lord Shiva caught Ganges in his hair as she cascaded down from heaven to the Himalayas. Ganges then followed Bhagiratha out of the mountains, across the plains to the sea, where she restored his dead ancestors and lifted them to paradise. As the Ganges brought to life the ashes of Bhagiratha's ancestors, so Hindus believe that if the ashes of their dead are deposited in the river their loved ones will be ensured a smooth transition to the next life—or even freed from the cycle of death and rebirth.

Washing clothes
in the Ganges
in Varanasi

Hindus may travel great distances to scatter the ashes of loved ones in the Ganges. Hindus also believe that Mother Ganges' divine waters purify those who immerse themselves in her. It is even said that a single drop of Ganges water, carried by the wind over a great distance, can cleanse a lifetime of sins. In cities along the river, daily dips are an important ritual among the faithful.

Many cities are considered sacred and serve as pilgrimage sites: Gangotri, where the river originates from a glacial cave; Sagar Island, where the Ganges drains into the sea and once restored the ancestors of Bhagiratha; Varanasi, the holiest of cities along the river's course and the most auspicious place to die; and Allahbad, the site of the most important festival in the Hindu religious calendar, Kumbh Mela. In 2001, some twenty million people bathed in the Ganges at Allahbad at the most auspicious moment of this festival.

But while her spiritual purity has remained unchallenged for millennia, Mother Ganges' physical purity has deteriorated as India's booming population imposes an ever-growing burden upon her. The river is now sick with the

Mt. Fuji seen from a distance

pollution of human and industrial waste, and water-borne illness is a terrible fact of Indian life.

Today the threat posed by this pollution isn't just a matter of health—it's a matter of faith. Veer Badra Mishra, a Hindu priest and civil engineer who has worked for decades to combat pollution in the Ganges, describes the importance of protecting this sacred river: "There is a saying that the Ganges grants us salvation. This culture will end if the people stop going to the river, and if the culture dies the tradition dies, and the faith dies." According to Mishra's view, to tell a Hindu that *Ganga*, goddess and mother, is "polluted" or "dirty" is an insult; it suggests that she is no longer sacred. Rather, the approach must acknowledge that human action, and not the holy river herself, is responsible: "We are allowing our mother to be defiled." This approach has stimulated grassroots involvement in a clean-up effort, and is transforming the work of environmental preservation into a model for cultural and religious preservation as well.

MOUNT FUJI Japan is one of the world's most mountainous countries, so it's not surprising that mountain worship is an element of Japanese cultural history. Of all the mountains in Japan, Mount Fuji stands out as a unique symbol: at 12,388 feet, Fuji is Japan's tallest mountain. Japan's two major religions, Shinto and Buddhism, regard Fuji as sacred. Japanese from all walks of life attest to the power of this natural symbol which is so deeply inscribed in the national psyche.

Mount Fuji is a composite volcano, growing larger as layer upon layer of lava and ash build up on its slopes. Like its geologic history, Mount Fuji's sacred history has also developed over time as different religions, beliefs, and myths have added new layers. Since ancient times, the mountains of Japan have been revered as sacred places, giving rise to a tradition of beliefs and rituals that scholars call *sangaku shinko*, "mountain creed."

When Shinto, the native religion of Japan, emerged sometime before the sixth century AD, it wove this mountain creed into a wider veneration of nature. According to Shinto belief, natural features such as trees, lakes, streams, rocks, and mountains are the dwelling places of spirits called *kami*. They influence human affairs and respond to human prayer and ritual. *Kami* are believed to be concentrated in mountain areas, and shrines have been erected to mark sacred spots.

The introduction of Buddhism from China in the sixth century further developed the practice of mountain worship. Buddhists, who viewed mountain climbing as a metaphor for spiritual ascent to enlightenment, adopted Shinto sacred mountains as pilgrimage destinations. In the ninth century, a religious sect called *Shugendo* arose. It based its doctrine and practice on mountain climbing itself, believing that practitioners could commune with deities on mountain summits and thereby obtain supernatural powers.

The name *Fuji* most likely came from an indigenous Ainu word meaning "deity of fire"—not surprising for a volcano that erupted often. Buddhists found in Fuji an inspiring symbol of meditation and called its summit *zenjo*, which is a Buddhist term describing a perfect meditative state. Buddhists also came to regard Fuji as the abode of the Buddha of All-Illuminating Wisdom. In the fourteenth century, *Shugendo* practitioners established the first climbing route to lead pilgrims to Fuji's summit. Four centuries later, Fuji-ko, societies devoted to the worship of Fuji became a major religious movement and inspired thousands of people to embark on annual pilgrimages. Those unable to make the climb used lava sand from the mountain to create miniature Fujis in home gardens and Shinto shrines.

CENTRAL AMERICA:
TIKAL, CHICHEN ITZA, AND THE MIRADOR BASIN

In the forests of Guatemala's El Petén region lie the ruined cities of one of the world's great ancient cultures, the Maya. The tops of stone pyramids rise over a dense jungle canopy teeming with wildlife and diverse plant species. The Mayan culture, which probably emerged around 1500 BC, made its mark on human history with an advanced civilization that stretched from Mexico's Yucatan Peninsula to northwestern Honduras and El Salvador. The Maya built large city-states, developed sophisticated agricultural techniques, created a hieroglyphic writing system, and used their advanced mathematical and astronomical knowledge to develop a precise calendar.

Some of their greatest cities lay in El Petén. This is a lowland tropical region in the northernmost part of Guatemala, bordering Mexico and comprising one-third of the country's territory. From AD 100 to 900, the cities of El Petén marked the height of Mayan civilization and distinguished the region as the "hearth" of the Mayan culture.

Like other indigenous peoples such as those of Peru and Australia, the Maya had a belief system rooted in reverence for nature. They believed in a supreme creator whose spirit is present in all living things. Nature took care of them, providing them with the means to farm, hunt, and stay healthy. They in turn had a responsibility to care for nature. Mayan spirituality was expressed through rituals performed in natural settings and at ancient Mayan cities and temples.

Nobel Prize-winning indigenous-rights activist Rigoberta Menchu explains: "The Mayas, our grandparents, always said: 'Every human being occupies a small piece of time.' Time itself is much longer, and because of this they always said that we must care for this earth while we are on it because it will be part of our children and the children of our grandchildren."

AFRICA: MOUNT KENYA Although it straddles the equator, Mount Kenya is usually capped with ice and snow. At 17,058 feet, it is Africa's second-highest mountain. Glaciers nest in its ragged peaks; forests blanket its slopes. This ancient extinct volcano, which rises in the center of the country that shares its name, has long been a wonder to all who have beheld its icy peaks gleaming with sunlight.

To the local African communities who live under it, Mount Kenya is not just an awesome sight but God's earthly home. It is a holy place, a cultural symbol, and a source of livelihood. To the Kikuyu, Bantu-speaking people who migrated to the foothills of Mount Kenya in the 1500s, the mountain is a sacred place and a central part of their creation myth.

According to tribal legend, their god *Ngai* created *Kirinyaga* (Mount Kenya), "the mountain of brightness," as an earthly dwelling place from which to survey his creation and bestow blessings and punishment upon his people. Many Kikuyu still retain traditional beliefs. In times of need such as drought, they turn toward *Kirinyaga* and perform ceremonies to *Ngai*. According to custom, Kikuyu homes are built with their doorways facing the mountain.

Other communities who live around the mountain, the Meru and Embu tribes, also revere Mount Kenya. Rituals are carried out in the mountain's sacred groves, and holy men make pilgrimages up the mountain. For all communities, Mount Kenya remains a strong cultural symbol.

USA SACRED SITES:

In the USA the sense of the sacred is built on the traditions of indigenous spiritual values. By reconnecting with invisible forces at various sites, we can regain our awareness of the sacredness of our land.

DEVILS TOWER, WYOMING Devils Tower, in northeastern Wyoming near the Black Hills of South Dakota, has been a location of spiritual significance for the Lakota people throughout their history. In June of each year, particularly important ceremonies connected to the summer solstice are held near the tower: these include pipe ceremonies, sun dances, and vision quests. Lakota elder Johnson Holy Rock says "If a man was starving, he was poor in spirit and in body, and he went into the Black Hills, the next spring he would come out, his life and body would be renewed. So, to our grandfathers, the Black Hills was the center of life, and those areas all around it were considered sacred and were kept in the light of reverence."

WOLF RIVER, WISCONSIN Protecting the purity of water in underground aquifers and surface streams is a deep spiritual responsibility held by the Sokaogon Chippewa and other native people in this region. According to Sokaogon beliefs, all water flowing on and under the ground is connected, and constitutes the lifeblood of *Nookomis oki*, Grandmother Earth. The Wolf River, its watershed, and the surrounding hill country have been used by generations of Sokaogon peoples for activities that pass on traditions and sustain their community's identity.

WEATHERMAN DRAW, MONTANA Weatherman Draw in south-central Montana is a valley that contains the largest collection of Native American rock art on the continent. Jimmy Arterberry, a Comanche preservation leader, explains that "this is a living spiritual center. The church is alive here."

The art in Weatherman Draw dates back over a thousand years and consists of multi-hued drawings of shields, animals, and human figures. Particularly intriguing are the shields that have heads and feet—perhaps representing specific individuals who can be traced from Mexico. Crow historian Howard Boggess writes that "the Art is alive and consecrated by the people who painted this work as they put their blood and sweat into each piece of work." It is also known as the "Valley of the Shields" or the "Valley of the Chiefs," and was historically a place of peace where many tribes—including the Comanche, Northern Arapaho, Northern Cheyenne, Eastern Shoshone, Crow, and

Devil's Tower in Wyoming figured prominently in Steven Spielberg's movie, Close Encounters of the Third Kind

Blackfeet—would gather in the winter. The valley was used for vision quests, burials, prayers, and for the gathering of medicinal plants.

PETROGLYPH NATIONAL MONUMENT, NEW MEXICO

Petroglyph National Monument is not just a national monument, but an area of great spiritual significance. "The petroglyph area is where messages to the spirit world are communicated. We consider each of these petroglyphs to be a record of visions written here of some spiritual being, event, or expression," says Bill Weahkee of the Five Sandoval Indian Pueblos.

The petroglyphs found in the area date back thousands of years. They are viewed by the various Pueblo groups as a place where messages are conveyed between ancestor spirits and the living. The ancestors chose this spot because of the dramatic alignment of five volcanoes—a place "born with Mother Earth's great labor and power," says Bill Weahkee. Since the first drawings were made on the rock, the petroglyph area has been used as a place for ceremonies, for gathering medicinal plants, and for offering thanks.

MAUNA KEA, HAWAII

Mauna Kea, a volcano on the island of Hawaii, is sacred to Native Hawaiians as an elder ancestor and the *kinolau* (physical embodiment) of deities revered in Hawaiian culture and religion. Mauna Kea is profoundly significant in Hawaiian culture and religion, representing the zenith of the Native Hawaiian people's ancestral ties to Creation itself.

In many oral histories throughout Polynesia, which pre-date modern science by millennia, the upper regions of Mauna Kea reside in *Wao Akua* (realm of the *Akua,* or Creator), and the summit is considered to be the temple of the Supreme Being. Mauna Kea is also the site of headwaters for the island of Hawaii. Modern Native Hawaiians continue to regard Mauna Kea with reverence and perform many cultural and religious practices there.

For Native Hawaiians, Mauna Kea is the home of *Na Akua* (the divine deities), *Na'Aumakua* (the divine ancestors), and the meeting place of *Papa* (Earth Mother) and *Wakea* (Sky Father), who are considered the progenitors of the Hawaiian people. Mauna Kea, it is said, is where the sky and earth separated to form the Great-Expanse-of-Space and the heavenly realms. Mauna Kea is both the burial ground and the embodiment of the most sacred ancestors, including *NaAli'i* and *Kahuna* (high ranking chiefs and priests).

The cinder cone Pu'u Hau'oki is one of three cinder cones that, together, were historically known as *Kukahau'ula. Kukahau'ula* is a male character who appears in recorded Hawaiian traditions and stories as the husband of *Lilinoe* and an *'aumakua* (family deity) of fishermen. *Lilinoe* is said to have been buried at the summit of Mauna Kea. She has been called "the woman of the mountain" and is known as the embodiment of fine mist—which is the literal meaning of her name.

SACRED PRACTICE TIME: WHERE IS YOUR HOLY LAND?

The earth's places have become largely interchangeable. Home lands are abandoned more and more as modern cultures value mobility; yet the conversation between our soul and the earth remains a dynamic one. In certain places one rediscovers the primordial, regenerative, and reciprocal bond between our soul and our earth. Personal healing may come about by redeeming our connection to the land, and by recognizing that the soul is deeply rooted in the earth.

The process of spiritually engaging with our physical environment evokes powerful feelings of peace. There is a deep sacredness associated with all forms of natural beauty; we may discover intimate connections to many places, creating new sanctuaries of our own. Sometimes the journey is made only in the imagination. Here are some ways to journey to your own sacred land.

DIG DOWN TO YOUR ROOTS Heritage and tradition are the threads that link us to the lands of our past, and one generation to another. Actively research your family's roots to discover the places on this earth that hold sacred meaning to you through this spiritual thread. Take notes and remember oral traditions. You might also utilize the Internet as well as specialists in the field of genealogical research.

JOURNEY TO YOUR ANCESTRAL ROOTS Bring your past into the present. Experience the towns and villages where your ancestors lived. Visit the buildings and churches which they knew, and walk in the fields, hills and valleys where they once walked. Walk the ground; walk on the bones of your ancestors. Once you've done that and know where your people come from, you can forge a connection with the land and the tradition.

CHAPTER EIGHT

GEOLOGY AND HEALING STONES

*"You will find something more in woods than in books.
Trees and stones will teach you that which you can
never learn from masters"*
—BERNARD OF CLAIRVAUX

WHEN YOU PICK UP a stone, you might think that it and all stones have remained the same since the beginning of the world. This is not the case. New stones are continually being formed. Other rocks are undergoing change.

Forces in nature, such as wind, water, gases, heat, and pressure are responsible for the chemical and physical changes in stones. These forces may affect stones on the surface of the earth or underground.

All stones can be placed into one of three broad categories:

SEDIMENTARY

IGNEOUS

METAMORPHIC

SEDIMENTARY

These are compressed silts, clays and sand composed of various minerals and often found inland near rivers. They are light, porous, and relatively young. Sedimentary rocks are created in four stages: erosion, transportation, deposition, and diagenesis.

Rocks exposed to water and air are constantly being changed by weathering and erosion. Rain, wind, and ice wear away small pieces of stone. Earthquakes, floods, glaciers, and people with bulldozers and dynamite remove

OPPOSITE: **Sandstone formation**

more. Wind sweeps away sand. Glaciers plow rocks in their path. Rain washes particles into low-lying areas and streams. As the rock fragments are tumbled about, the edges are ground smooth. You can see rounded pebbles and rocks when you wade in a creek. Your feet stir up silt and sediment on the bottom. These fragments can travel a long way. For example, rock eroded from the Grand Canyon in Arizona can be carried down the Colorado River to the Gulf of California, about four hundred miles away. Eventually, some of the material goes all the way to the ocean.

Stones are constantly undergoing change

Deposition is the laying down of material when it finally stops moving. One layer after another is deposited in the same place. The weight of the layers presses out water and squeezes the materials together. Minerals in the water, such as silica, carbonates, and iron oxides then cement the particles into rock. This process is called diagenesis.

Sedimentary rocks are not formed only from rock fragments. Shells, minerals, and organic matter can also build up in layers and over time these can become rock as well.

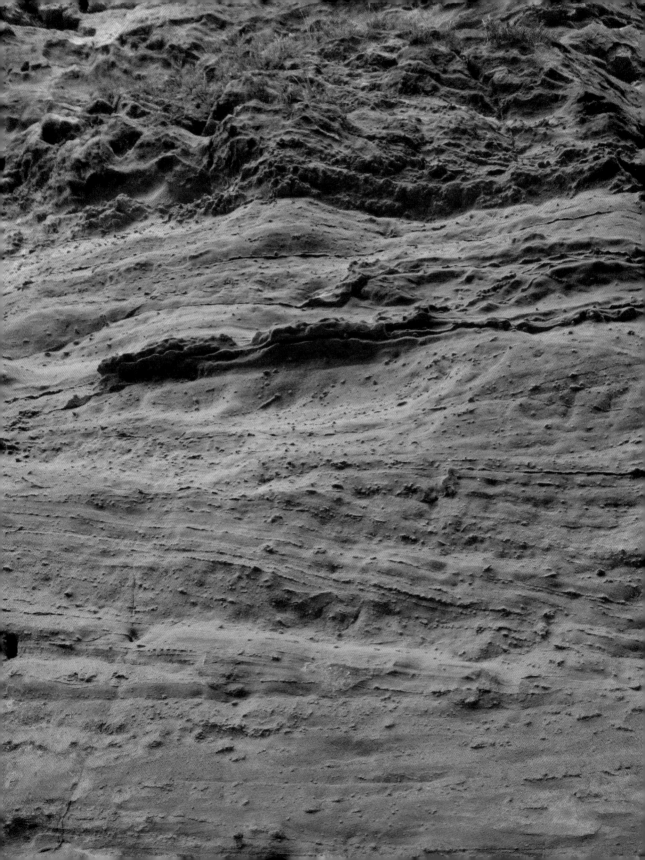

"Puddingstone" is a common name given to a conglomerate sedimentary rock that has distinct round pebbles suspended like cherries in Jell-O. A conglomerate is a mass of different objects stuck together. The fine material between the larger objects is called the matrix. The smoothness of the particles in the puddingstone indicates that the small rocks were tumbled in water before they settled and cemented into a conglomerate.

Sandstone is made up of grains of sand adhering together. Sandstone feels gritty when you rub it. Its color and strength depend on the material that cements it together. Sandstone may be yellow, brown, red, gray or green. The presence of iron oxide gives it a rusty hue, while cobalt, nickel and titanium result in richer colors. Silica provides the strongest cement. Shale has the smallest particles of all sedimentary rocks. Shale is made from clay or mud. It forms in hollows containing dissolved quartz in water.

Obsidian

IGNEOUS

Igneous means "made by fire." These rocks form when hot melted rock, or magma, cools. Igneous rocks can form above or below ground. Once magma comes out of the earth it is called lava. Where and how fast it cools and its mineral composition are major factors determining which type of igneous rock magma becomes.

There are two major types of magma: basaltic magma and rhyolitic magma. Each type of lava has a different mineral composition, so they form different types of rock.

Basaltic magma erupts quietly and flows easily. It forms from volcanoes with gently sloping sides, and can quickly flow over a large area.

Rhyolitic magma erupts explosively, releasing a blast of lava and gas. Rhyolitic

Natural basalt formation

magma doesn't flow very easily, so it forms volcanoes with steep sides. The explosive eruptions can also propel some rhyolitic magma far from the volcano.

There are two main types of igneous rocks.

INTRUSIVE

EXTRUSIVE

As each type of magma cools, extrusive rocks form. There are three well-known examples of extrusive igneous rock.

OBSIDIAN

PUMICE

BASALT

OBSIDIAN is a volcanic glass that forms when lava is thrown into the air. It is generally black but can be gray or streaked with reddish brown. It cools and hardens so rapidly that crystals don't have time to grow; thus it becomes a smooth, dark glassy stone.

Obsidian occasionally forms as long filaments called "Pele's Hair." These clumps of golden brown strands look like glassy wire. Pele is the legendary goddess of volcanic fire from the Hawaiian tradition.

PUMICE is an extrusive igneous rock formed primarily from explosive rhyolitic eruptions. When a gas-filled mass of lava is spewed into the air, the gas bubbles, called vesicules, expand, and the frothy lava cools and hardens into pumice. This rock, which usually is light in color, looks like frozen foam. In fact the name pumice comes from the Latin word meaning foam.

BASALT is a type of rock that forms when basaltic lava flows out of a volcano and covers the surrounding land. Basalt, like obsidian, is generally black. However, over time it can change to brown or red when the iron in the basalt oxidizes. Oxidization occurs when a substance chemically combines oxygen. A form of oxidization that you're probably familiar with is rust, which forms on iron metal. Basalt is by far the most widespread extrusive igneous rock.

After repeated eruptions and lava flows, basalt can accumulate to incredible thicknesses—many thousands of feet—and can cover thousands of square miles. In fact, a layer of basalt lies beneath all the ocean floors, which make up two-thirds of the earth's surface. Such massive beds of cooled lava are called flood basalts. The buildup of basalt from underwater volcanoes can also create island chains, such as the Hawaiian Islands.

METAMORPHIC

Just as a butterfly goes through metamorphosis while changing from a caterpillar, stones also can be changed over time. *Meta* means "change" and *morph* means "form." Metamorphic rocks are completely changed from the original stone in structure, ionic activity, and appearance. Metamorphic rocks form when igneous and sedimentary rocks are exposed to great heat and pressure.

High temperatures can be caused by nearby magma, hot gases, or simply the intense pressure deep within the earth—where pressure results from the weight of the earth above, or movement of the plates within, the earth's crust.

The high temperatures and intense pressure can cause physical and chemical changes to occur in rock. In addition to changing the existing texture and mineral composition of the rock, sometimes new elements are introduced by hot liquids and gases that flow beneath the earth. The new metamorphic rock can differ in color, hardness, and texture from the original rock, which is called the protolith.

Most change occurs over a long period of time. However, a cataclysmic event such as the impact of a meteorite can also produce extremely high temperatures and pressures. In such cases, surrounding rocks can change almost instantly. This type of metamorphism is called "shock metamorphism."

Marble is a metamorphic stone which starts out as limestone. Under heat and pressure, the calcite within the limestone recrystallizes and forms large, coarse grains. Pure marble is white, but other colors are common when impurities such as clay minerals are present. The colors can have a veined effect when the impurities are swirled throughout the rock. Colors can include buff, yellow, pink, red, green, gray, and black.

GEOMAGNETISM

According to physical science, there are essentially two types of magnetism. The natural magnetic energy of the earth, or geomagnetism, is diffuse but constant. It operates in a gigantic field, whereas the magnetism produced by dipole magnets and electromagnets has stronger intensity but is more limited in scope.

The origin of geomagnetism is still not known. However, magnetism ultimately underlies all of earthly nature from rocks and plants to humans and their brains. Part of the earth's magnetic field is generated internally; geophysicists believe that most of the earth's iron is concentrated in the planet's core.

The earth can be considered a giant permanent magnet with two poles whose origins are both internal and external. The external influence is thought to arise from ionization of the layers surrounding the earth.

The earth's geomagnetic field is subject to slow variations, which are neither uniform nor constant. The intensity of the geomagnetic field can increase in one region of the globe and decrease, irregularly, in another. These variations originate from the interior of the earth as well as in response to electromagnetic currents in the ionosphere.

OPPOSITE: *Flowing water shaping stone*

STONE: NATURAL PERMANENT MAGNETS

Experts have established that in the last seventy million years the earth's magnetic field has reversed itself more than a hundred times. Like many of the earth's invisible rhythms, these field reversals are typically slow, taking from five to seven thousand years to complete. Strong evidence of this phenomena first emerged in the 1950s and 1960s, when scientists towing magnetic sensors behind ships found that the rocky seabed exhibited odd stripes of magnetization.

Scientists found that continuous flows of seabed lava had become alternately magnetized over the ages as the polarities of the earth's field switched first one way, then the other. The seabed acted like a huge tape recorder, and the same proved true of the layered deposits of old volcanoes on land.

Ancient molten lava held tiny mineral grains that acted like innumerable compasses, or miniature magnets, freely aligning themselves with the contemporary field. As the lava cooled the tiny compasses froze in place, immobile even when the field shifted once again. Experts called it paleomagnetism. They found that the tiny compasses were often made of magnetite, a naturally magnetic mineral.

Flowing lava on Kona, the big island of Hawaii

It can therefore be said that stones are natural permanent magnets. The first magnets noticed and used by humans were magnets of this type of volcanic origin. When lava emerges from a volcano it cools gradually, locking in the earth's magnetism. When the lava has completely cooled, it forms a stone that has absorbed a certain amount of the magnetic energy of the earth. However, it is the iron (ore) content of volcanic stone that determines its magnetic power, as well as its durability as a heat-retaining agent in stone massage. All non-specific stones are carriers of geomagnetism. The effect is subtle yet powerful and has been known for millennia.

Iceland spar

METAPHYSICS
AND STONE LORE

In ancient lore, stone has been a universal metaphor for integrity and durability. Stones were also used as a mystical symbol of hidden blessings and treasures of the earth, as in the story in the Bible of water springing from rock when struck by the rod of Moses.

According to ancient historians, stones—being of the earth—represented the feminine energy in general. Small stones dating back to the Paleolithic Period thirty thousand years ago were carved with full breasts and swelling bellies, personifying the earth as mother goddess. It is thought that they may have been held in the hand or placed upon an altar in worship, as icons of the mother goddess.

Non-specific stones found in nature, at the seashore or along river beds, are unique and individual, with minerals and ores in beautiful arrangements. Some stones look like they have been created by a sculptor or colored by an artist. They are especially colorful when wet. If you look closely at stones, you will see that each one has subtle color variations.

Here are some thoughts pertaining to the meaning of color and ores in stones.

GREEN STONES   Green in any stone is almost always a synonym for continuous vitality, partly through its connection to the hope of renewal. In Chinese culture, jade, a green stone, has an elevated value and is associated with virtues of purity, justice, truth, harmony, and loyalty. Green is also said to keep love constant.

The green colors are imparted by the presence of coppers and copper sulfites. Copper is a conductor of electromagnetism. When energy is stopped or blocked at any point in the body, difficulties can develop. Amplification of the human energy field via magnetism can help promote circulation to the extremities and detoxification of the bloodstream.

Copper-rich stones may be helpful in rheumatoid arthritis and tension reduction. They retain heat for long periods, which makes them useful in heated-stone therapy.

Malachite

WHITE STONES; QUARTZITE, AND MARBLE It is believed that white stone has an affinity for bones, teeth, and nails, and that it augments the body's ability to assimilate minerals and other nutrients used in the formation of skeletal tissue. White stones are generally used cool in body therapy as they do not retain heat at all. They help the body to contain fluid in certain conditions, which can aid in reducing excessive heat or dryness and in balancing body temperature. White stones may be lightly brushed over the face in facial massage to drain puffiness and to relieve tension headache by redirection of excess mental energy away from the head and downward into the body.

GRANITE AND ROSE GRANITE Granite works especially well on the first three chakras, helping balance and align the areas below and including the solar plexus chakra by grounding mental energies. The benefits of being grounded will be seen in areas of finance, addiction, and stress. Granite brings vitality to the weaker parts of the body.

BLACK AND DARK GREY STONES These are stones of substance. They provide a sense of security, addressing first chakra security and survival issues. Iron, because of its association with early weapons and with fire itself, has been considered to have protective properties. In ancient Egypt, it was endowed with talismanic value. Views like this may account for the protective symbolism of nails, and for curious customs in some cultures such as hammering additional nails into a house post to drive away bad spirits. The Romans ceremonially drove a nail into a wall of Jupiter's temple each September as insurance against disaster.

In massage and energy healing therapies, black stones, containing iron ore, are the densest and most durable heat-delivery agents. Used warm or hot they strengthen and tone air-filled organs and cavities. They are especially

Mica

helpful to the lungs, the thyroid, and the central nervous system because they reduce air and ether in the system.

RED OR RUST-COLORED STONES, INCLUDING PURPLE AND FOLIATED STONES

Among stones, the ruby is valued by Indian traditions as a promoter of longevity and health. Red-colored stone imparts regenerative properties, especially to

Spinel

the bloodstream, since red stone acts to purify the blood. It also strongly affects the sex drive by strengthening the emotions of the heart and by linking actions to the heart. It correlates to the planet Mars and the sun, governing passion and generosity. Red stones can steady mental energies while promoting concentration, so they are helpful in meditation. Red stone acts as shield and protector, safeguarding the psyche and the unconscious from intrusion and distraction. In Hindu culture, a dot of ground paste of red sandalwood is worn at the pineal chakra on the *bindi* point.

PINK OR ROSE-COLORED STONES

Pink stones promote inner peace and serenity. Pinks are cooling, nurturing, and sustaining, blending the properties of the white quartzites and the reds. Pinks in general have a beneficial effect on the

Kunzite

endocrine system and the corresponding chakras and their diaphragms, releasing tension, contraction, and negativity. Often, there will be a detoxifying and cathartic event in association with the pink stones. Pink is said to heal the primal wound. (This is that wound we were born with, which has nothing to do with the parenting or acculturation we did or did not receive.) Pink heals this with the promotion of perspective and self love.

PRACTICE: USING BIRTHSTONES FOR PERSONAL BALANCE

The concept of "birth" stones originated from the Indian studies of astrology and cosmology. Crystals and gemstones are composed of clear and purified minerals which also are present in the human body. According to Harish Johari in *The Healing Power of Gemstones*, "[all] stones absorb and produce specific energies that are related to the frequencies of the light they receive." Some healers in the ancient traditions suggest wearing certain colored stones as talismans to conduct energy from the earth and to provide strength to "weak" planets in a person's birth chart. Certainly these practices are tied to the notion that the human body is composed of the same minerals present in the earth.

The light frequencies, or energies, are related to planetary energies that go well beyond the ordinary visible spectrum. They may serve to conduct or amplify electromagnetic and geomagnetic energy which, in turn, influence the electrochemical nature of the body. Healing gemstones work with physiological energy as well as subtle energy whether worn as jewelry or used in other forms. Traditionally, there is a gemstone that correlates to each of the powerful planets as follows.

PLANET	STONE	COLOR	PROPERTY
THE SUN	Ruby	Red	Strengthens the heart
THE MOON	Pearl	Silver White, Translucent	Cools inflammation
JUPITER	Yellow Sapphire	Gold	Bestows good fortune
MERCURY	Emerald	Green	Calms the nerves
VENUS	Diamond	Clear	Durability of love
MARS	Coral	Red	Tonic

Here is a quick way to decide which crystal or gemstone may be beneficial for you. This method takes into account the planet governing, or rising above, the horizon at the time of your birth, rather than the sun's sign of the zodiac. Ancient medical astrology links the rising or ascending sign to the physical body.

RISING SIGN AT BIRTH	RULING PLANET	COLOR	STONES FOR BALANCE	STONES TO STRENGTHEN
ARIES	Mars	Red	Pearl	Ruby/Coral
TAURUS	Venus	Green	Diamond	Emerald
GEMINI	Mercury	Clear/Yellow	Emerald	Diamond
CANCER	Moon	White/Silver	Ruby	Pearl/Silver
LEO	Sun	Red/Gold	Pearl/Silver	Gold/Ruby
VIRGO	Mercury	Green/White	Emerald	Diamond
LIBRA	Venus	Green	Diamond	Emerald
SCORPIO	Mars/Pluto	Red/Black	Pearl	Blue Sapphire
SAGGITARIUS	Jupiter	Yellow/Blue	Diamond	Yellow Saphire
CAPRICORN	Saturn	Blue/Black	Ruby/Coral	Blue Sapphire
AQUARIUS	Uranus/Saturn	Blue/Black	Blue/Sapphire	Ruby/Coral
PISCES	Neptune/Jupiter	Blue/Silver	Coral	Pearl/Silver

CHAPTER NINE

FIELD GUIDE TO HEALING STONES

"And then our life, exempt from public haunt,
Finds tongues in trees, books in the running brooks
Sermons in stones, and food in everything."
—SHAKESPEARE, *AS YOU LIKE IT*

MASSAGE STONES 101

USING HEATED STONES in massage can have powerful healing effects. The composition of a massage stone determines its "thermal radiance potential," or how long a stone will radiate *consistent* gentle warmth. Stones with high iron ore content possess geomagnetic remanence. The combination of energy and heat-delivery qualities will amplify the potency of any body therapy you offer. Preferences in size and type of stone abound and vary from person to person.

When looking for stones to use in warm stone massage, there are four important criteria: composition, shape, texture and size.

Composition tells you how much and what kind of mineral and ore content there are in a stone. Ore is a thermal and geomagnetic conductor. The greater the ore content, the heavier the stone. Look and feel for density.

Shape refers to comfort in layouts. Look for stones that fit the natural contours of the body.

Texture refers to a stone's capacity to stimulate inert lymph fluid in massage stroking. Look for varied textures; avoid collecting only smooth and polished stones.

Size refers to weight and traction benefits. Size also refers to the length of time for consistent heat delivery: a big stone stays warm longer than a small one. For body work, look for stones at least as big as your palm, including the length of your fingers. Weight is also an integral and desired feature of larger stones. For example, placement of the large belly or organ stone applies warm, direct, sustained pressure against the inner breathing movement. This exerts an internal massage and flushing action to certain visceral ducts, especially at the important gall bladder and liver region.

STONE COLORS

The thermal radiance potential of a stone is based upon how much ore is in the stone. Ores impart varying colors: pale green, grey, rust, blue, buff, and black; they are not all smooth and black. It is a myth that black stones hold heat better or longer than light-colored stones. Stones should never be polished or mechanically tumbled. After repeated immersion in oils and water, your massage stones will develop a beautiful rich dark patina. They appear lighter in color when you find them in nature.

Water brings out the colors in stones.

UNIVERSAL SHAPES FOUND IN STONES

 a. **Round**
(used in layout)

 b. **Oblong**
(used in belly/back layouts)

 c. **Triangular**
(used under/over sacrum/heart)

 d. **Heart-Shaped**
(used over thymus/heart)

 e. **Liver-Shaped**
(used in visceral layout)

 f. **Kidney-Shaped**
(used in foundation layout under kidneys)

 g. **Cylindrical**
(used as a neck roll under neck)

 h. **Half-Sphere**
(used as hand rests)

 i. **Conical**
(inserted between scapulas/under neck/over trapezius)

SEDIMENTARY

These can be very beautiful in appearance with multi-hued layers and foliations made of minerals and other inclusions. However, these are not the most durable stones. Generally lacking a core of iron ore, they do not hold heat for very long and are not consistent heat-delivery stones.

IGNEOUS

Ninety percent of commercial massage stones are igneous. These stones must be used with caution due to their potential for extreme surface temperatures and thermal inconsistency. They heat up quickly and cool down just as quickly, making them most suitable for use in moving strokes over the surface anatomy—in contrast to the layout stones, which stay in one place on the body for twenty minutes or longer.

METAMORPHIC

Sold by small companies who harvest stones by hand for massage practitioners, metamorphic stones are the best choice for heated stone therapy. Due to their high ore content, metamorphic stones retain heat consistently. Used in core-body thermal compress applications, they tend to retain warmth for twenty to thirty minutes.

Beach Marble

Beach marble stones may be sea-smoothed milky quartzite, or a combination of milky quartzite and marble. They do not retain heat at all.

ESTABLISHING A SACRED RELATIONSHIP WITH STONES

Perhaps as important as the stones that you'll collect is the location that they are "harvested" from. In order for a stone to possess the exact combination of requirements needed for use in bodywork, it will have to be from a place in nature that is clean and healthy environmentally. Therefore search at the very tip of ocean peninsulas and along rivers with white rapids. The stones found in inlets, bays, and the tidal pools around marshes are usually covered with algae and rough edges, even though they may be beautiful and ore-rich.

A NOTE ABOUT COMMERCIAL STONES You now can find healing massage stones for sale at discount warehouses and on Internet websites. It is easy for us to feel removed from nature in the acquisition of commercial massage stones. They have often been taken from the earth without reverence, in an ungrateful way. Nothing has been given back in return for earth's treasures.

You can give back the consciousness lacking in the chain of delivery of such stones if you value them, love them, care for them, and use them fully for their purpose, thanking the earth from which they came. Ideally, when they are shining with the patina of having served and been cared for, you will then pass your healing stones on. Or, you will restore them to their original source by burying them, allowing them once again to become the body of the earth mother.

Tribal Native American elders and medicine keepers consider all rocks to be part of the clan of the stone people, and they believe that stones have souls.

Natives of the Americas consider stones to be "record keepers," which help us remember lost truth or receive divine vision.

These people understand that for every process they put a natural object through, they must make up for its loss of aliveness by replacing it with some of their own. For example if they change a stone's integrity with polishing and shaping, they must add their loving desire to create according to an inspired vision. In other words, they put their blessing into each object or act of creation.

It is in the same manner that we will gather our healing stones, with the spiritual agreement to serve, adding our love every step of the way. Your stones are precious things, whether you hand-harvest them yourself or have a collection which has accumulated from many sources over the years.

Your power—and that of healing stones—comes from your love for them and from your use of them with pure heartfelt consciousness. Any object can empower you if you treat it as an entity with whom you have a relationship. If an object has not been taken from earth or utilized respectfully, you must understand that it will deplete you over time. This is the circle of life. There is no receiving without giving. Loving care of anything is what keeps it, and you, going.

Here is an excerpt from a story about the healing power of stones, told by Grey Wolf, grandson of a Lakota Medicine Man and spiritual healer.

When I was a boy, I noticed that my grandfather always had a stone in his pocket. It seemed strange to me for an old man always to be carrying a stone with him. The way I got to notice the stone was that whenever my grandfather was saying his prayers, or healing, or counseling, even when he was just deep in thought, out came the stone. If he was working with someone who had come to him, quite often he would take their hand and get them to hold his stone while he performed his medicine. On one occasion, a man came to him in a lot of pain. He had been working with his horses when he wrenched his shoulder badly. Although not dislocated, it was very badly bruised and he could hardly move it. My grandfather began massaging it. After a while, he took his stone out of his pocket and rolled it between his own hand and all over the man's neck, down his back, up over his shoulder, and down his arm. When he was finished, the man raised his arm up, and you could tell that the pain was gone.

All this fascinated me, and I asked my grandfather about the stone. It was a small piece of agate, nothing spectacular, just rather rounded. He explained to me about Inyan, the stone people or rock spirits, who are the oldest living

OPPOSITE: **The healing powers of stones depend upon the care you invest in them**

beings upon the earth. They are actually closer to Mother Earth in physical form than any of the rest of her children. Inyan hold knowledge and power century after century; to them a decade is like a second of our lives. The knowledge, wisdom, and power that the stone people hold is the strongest of all the peoples.

My grandfather told me that each human being has their own stone or watai. Just as all humans have animals that help them, so too Inyan, the stone people, form relationships with humans. It is recognized in the name watai—a link between the seen and unseen worlds. [3]

According to Native American traditions rocks are living beings and belong to the Clan of the Stone People

The Native American traditions teach that your special stone will find you. It will come to you and show itself. It will cause you to have to pick it up. Once you have found your *watai*, or medicine stone, you will discover that it continues to get your attention in very subtle ways. For example, it may begin to heat up for no apparent reason. This may be a signal to listen internally for a message from your own higher consciousness. Often, you may remember your misplaced power and strength in this way.

PRACTICE: STONE MEDITATION FOR FOCUS AND MANIFESTATION OF DREAMS

You may use a single pebble or small stone that feels good to you as a talisman to assist in focusing your ambitions or dreams. Hold the stone or pebble in your right hand and focus your attention on its qualities.

With your eyes closed, feel the grain of its surface texture and the cool hardness against your palm. Wrap your entire hand around the stone and notice how your body heat merges with the cool surface, and then moves more deeply into the core of the stone. Now squeeze the stone tightly in your hand as you wish for the fulfillment of one single, clear, important dream or goal. Choose only one goal; remember, this is a discipline in grounding.

As you do so, imagine that the stone is glowing inside of your palm, charged with the energy and power of your wish.

Now, place the stone in a place where you will see it on a daily basis to remind you of your intention. Whenever you are about to take a step toward your goal and require an extra boost, squeeze the stone in your hand to focus your mind and harness your internal energies.

Walking on cobblestones stimulates reflexology points.

PRACTICE: A SIMPLE EXERCISE TO TAP INTO EARTH'S VITAL ENERGY

ROCK WALKING FOR HEALTHFUL AND GRACEFUL AGING While it may be accepted in the western world that a necessary consequence of aging is declining health, that is not necessarily the case in some Asian cultures.

Based on the preponderance of healthy and animated Chinese elders, many Chinese practices have been studied and incorporated into healthy lifestyles in the West. Chinese herbs, acupuncture, *qi gong, tai chi* and meditation are some of the healthful customs we have adopted. Now there is scientific evidence that one more Chinese tradition contributes to healthful and graceful aging.

It is common to observe people exercising, dancing, and walking back and forth over traditional stone paths in China. Behavioral researchers from the Oregon Research Institute undertook a study to determine if there were health benefits of walking on these rocks. According to an Associated Press report on July 12, 2005 by William McCall, "[t]he path to better health and lower blood pressure may be paved with cobblestones." This study showed that when people over the age of sixty walked on smooth, rounded cobblestones for just a half an hour a day over four months, they significantly lowered their blood pressure and improved their balance.

Walking on rocks likely stimulates reflexology and acupressure points on the feet. These are points to which distant and seemingly unrelated areas of the body are linked. This comes as no surprise to practitioners and proponents of these systems of massage. According to acupuncture (or acupressure) meridian theory, the kidney channel begins on the sole of the foot. Stimulation of this area, known as Kidney 1 or "Gushing Spring," is said to bring excess energy down from the head. This has the physiological effect of lowering blood pressure.

Fay Horak, an Oregon Health and Science University neurophysiologist who specializes in balance, said the study is evidence that finding ways to maintain mobility and balance can delay and even prevent the effects of aging. According to Horak, "[the] body relies on two complex methods to maintain balance: the vestibular system in the inner ear and the somatosensory system that connects skin and muscles." When the ground is uneven, the body relies more on the vestibular system in the inner ear for balance control. As we age, we lose receptors in the inner ear. This is one of the contributing factors to the increase in falls among the elderly.

When the challenge of walking on rocks, an uneven surface, is presented, subjects use the working portion of their vestibular system. Horak suggests that challenging the vestibular system is even likely to improve its function.

Proof of improving balance and lowering blood pressure is significant. While walking on rocks may not be a "fountain of youth," it is a practice that can enhance the quality of life.

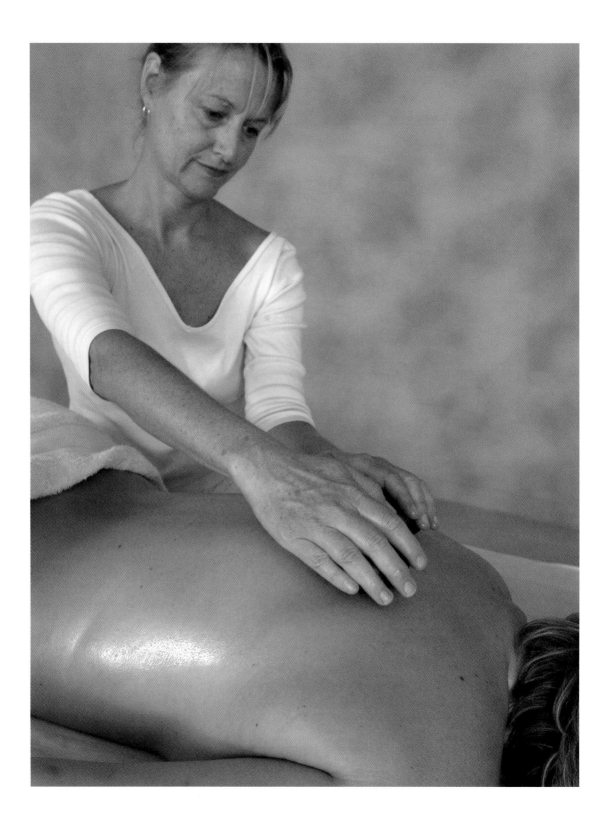

CHAPTER TEN

Massage
and Healing

MASSAGE IS ONE OF the oldest healing arts: Chinese records dating back three thousand years document its use; the ancient Hindus, Persians, and Egyptians applied forms of massage for many ailments; and Hippocrates recommended the use of rubbing and friction for joint and circulatory problems.

Today, the benefits of massage are known to be varied and far-reaching. As an accepted part of many physical rehabilitation programs, massage therapy has proven beneficial for many chronic conditions, including low back pain, arthritis, bursitis, fatigue, high blood pressure, diabetes, immunity suppression, infertility, smoking cessation, depression, and more. And, as many millions will attest, massage also helps relieve the stress and tension of everyday living, which can lead to disease and illness.

THE BENEFITS OF MASSAGE

Massage provides relief to people of all ages—from infants to seniors—and from all walks of life including the weekend or competitive athlete, the home gardener, and the overstressed, overworked executive.

Treating the Four Pillars of Your Health with Massage

Massage therapy improves all four pillars of well-being. It provides food, or nourishment, through the skin; restorative relaxation and meditative brain patterning; passive and remedial exercise; and tremendous sensory pleasure. It addresses a variety of health conditions, the most prevalent being stress-related tension, which, experts believe, accounts for eighty to ninety percent of disease. Massage has been proven beneficial in treating cancer-related fatigue, sleep disorders, high blood pressure, diabetes, low back pain, immunity suppression, spinal cord injury, autism, post-operative conditions, age-related disorders, infertility, eating disorders, smoking cessation, and depression, to name just a few.

Here's why: massage offers a drug-free, non-invasive, and humanistic approach based on the body's natural ability to heal itself. Massage has many beneficial physiological effects, such as the following.

- *Increasing circulation, allowing the body to pump more oxygen and nutrients into tissues and vital organs*

- *Stimulating the lymph system, the body's natural defense against toxic invaders; for example, in breast cancer patients, massage has been shown to increase the cells that fight cancer*

- *Relaxing and softening injured and overused muscles*

- *Reducing spasms and cramping*

- *Increasing joint flexibility*

- *Reducing recovery time for people who do strenuous workouts; eliminating subsequent pain for the athlete of any level*

- *Releasing endorphins, the body's natural painkiller; for this reason, massage is being incorporated into treatment for injuries, chronic illness, and recovery from surgery*

- *Reducing post-surgery adhesions and edema, and reducing and realigning scar tissue after healing has occurred*

- *Improving range of motion and decreasing discomfort for patients with low back pain*

- *Relieving pain for migraine sufferers, decreasing the need for medication*

- *Providing exercise and stretching for atrophied muscles; reducing the shortening of muscles for those with restricted range of motion*

SO WHAT IS IT EXACTLY?

Massage therapies are defined as the application of various manual techniques to the muscular structure and soft tissues of the human body; specifically, the application of manipulation techniques intended to reduce stress and fatigue while improving circulation.

There are many different kinds of massage therapies and techniques. The application of these techniques may include but is not limited to stroking, kneading, tapping, compression, vibration, rocking, friction, and pressure. Techniques may also include non-forceful passive or active movement, and application of techniques intended to affect the energetic systems of the body. The use of oils, lotions, and heat may also be included.

HEALING AND WARM STONE MASSAGE

These techniques are gaining popularity all over the world, but massage with heat is not new at all. It is an integration of many approaches to massage and healing. What is new is the creativity: therapists now combine aromatherapy oils, heated stones and crystals with massage. It is written in ancient texts that the earth provides a remedy for every condition at the time the disease is discovered. The deep inner calm provided by massage with warm stones is a wonderful medicine for today's fast-paced living.

HEALING STONE MASSAGE INTEGRATES MANY FORMS

ACUPRESSURE   Michael Reed Gach, director of the Acupressure Institute, defines acupressure in his book *Acupressure's Potent Points* as follows.

> "Acupressure is an ancient healing art that uses the fingers to press key points on the surface of the skin to stimulate the body's natural self-curative abilities. When these points are pressed, they release muscular tension and promote the circulation of blood and the body's life force (sometimes known as *qi* or *chi*) to aid healing. Acupuncture and acupressure use the same points, but acupuncture employs needles, while acupressure uses the gentle, but firm pressure of hands (and even feet).
>
> Acupressure can be effective in helping relieve headaches, eye strain, sinus problems, neck pain, backaches, arthritis, muscle aches, tension due to stress, ulcer pain, menstrual cramps, lower backaches, constipation, and indigestion.
>
> The origins of acupressure are as ancient as the instinctive impulse to hold your forehead or temples when you have a headache. Everyone at one time or another has used their hands spontaneously to hold tense or painful places on the body." [4]

AROMATHERAPY The use of essential oils—which are extracted from herbs, flowers, resin, woods, and roots—in body and skin care treatments is known as aromatherapy. Used in antiquity by the Egyptians, Greeks, and Romans, essential oils aid in relaxation, improve circulation, and help the healing of wounds. Specific essential oils are blended and added to a carrier oil such as almond oil and are used during the massage. Each of the oils has its own unique characteristics and benefits.

AYURVEDIC MASSAGE An Ayurvedic massage is one part of the traditional detoxification and rejuvenation program of India called *panchakarma,* in which the entire body is vigorously massaged with large amounts of warm oil and herbs to remove toxins from the system. These treatments are powerful in their effects upon the mind and nervous system, calming, balancing, and bringing forth a heightened sense of awareness and deep inner peace. The basis for effectively performing all of the various Ayurvedic massage techniques is a thorough understanding of the primordial energies of the five elements: ether, air, fire, water, and earth.

BALNEOTHERAPY The ancient use of waters and clays to restore and revitalize the body is known as balneotherapy. It has been used to improve circulation, fortify the immune system, relieve pain, and treat stress.

CHI NEI TSANG This technique was created by a Taoist monk over two thousand years ago in the mountain monasteries of China. In order for the monks to be able to learn to perform the highest levels of spiritual practice, they needed to generate a very high level of energy. Today, *chi nei tsang* is still practiced for this same reason, but people in all walks of life who seek greater health and well-being can use it. *Chi* means "energy" and "information," and *nei tsang* means "viscera" or "internal organs." *Chi nei tsang* addresses the origins of health problems including psychosomatic responses. It also increases the resilience of the body's defense system. *Chi nei tsang* focuses mainly on the abdomen, with deep, soft, gentle touch helping to train internal organs to work more efficiently. All the body systems are addressed: digestive, respiratory, lymphatic, nervous, endocrine, urinary, reproductive, and so on. *Chi nei tsang* integrates applied *qi gong* with the art of abdominal massage.

DEEP TISSUE ATHLETIC MASSAGE Techniques which utilize deep tissue and deep muscle massage are incorporated to affect the musculature and connective tissues. These techniques require advanced training and a thorough understanding of anatomy and physiology. Muscles must be relaxed in order for deep tissue massage to be effective; otherwise tight surface muscles prevent the practitioner from reaching the deeper musculature. Deep athletic tissue massage helps with chronic muscular pain and injury rehabilitation and reduces inflammation-related pain caused by arthritis and tendonitis. It is integrated with other massage techniques.

EARTH ENERGY AND STONE HEALING This technique involves laying stones upon and around the body. It is similar to Reiki as it is the channeling of energy and also entails laying on of the hands.

ENERGY FLOW BALANCING This gentle treatment assists in balancing energy flow. The practitioner holds a space for the recipient to make whatever shifts or changes toward balance he or she may deem necessary. Emphasis is given to the chakras and the joints, leaving the recipient feeling at peace and at home with themselves—with less pain, increased mobility, and greater range of motion.

ESOTERIC HEALING This is a healing through the energy field, which flows through and around us and our chakras, or centers of energy. Each of the seven major centers vitalizes its related endocrine gland or glands. It is possible to interpret the energy field associated with each chakra, and to assist in the restoration of good health through rebalancing the energy field as a whole.

Massage practitioners learn to sensitize their hands and inner perception to examine the energy field in detail in order to find alterations in the flow of energy. The recipient remains fully clothed.

FOOT ZONE THERAPY Foot zone therapy is based on the premise that energy flows through the body in meridians from the brain to the feet. Every organ and cell has a representative point on the foot. When pressure is applied, the brain sends a signal to the corresponding part of the body, facilitating healing and restoring balance. Temporary pain, defined also as a blockage of energy flow, is felt on areas of the foot which correspond to the affected organ or body part. When the pain is relieved or reduced, the healing process has begun.

GEOMAGNETIC THERAPY Originally involving a stone called magnetite applied in a poultice, the therapeutic use of magnets may be older than acupuncture. Today's geomagnetic therapy is still applied to the skin in the form of stones. Geomagnetic therapy is used to relieve pain and discomfort and to aid in healing a variety of physical and emotional disorders such as arthritis and stress. Geomagnetic therapy principles utilize the diffuse magnetic energy within stones, rather than the more focused dipole magnet effect.

HOLISTIC MEDICINE Holistic medicine recognizes that the mind, spirit, lifestyle, environment, and other aspects of a person's existence significantly affect the functioning of the physical body. In its evaluation and treatment of symptoms and its recommendations for preventing illness, this approach treats the whole person, addressing more than just the symptoms or disease.

ORIENTAL MASSAGE Monitoring the flow of the vital life energy known as *chi, ki,* or *prana* is at the heart of Oriental massage. Using physical pressure and manipulation, the healer evaluates and modulates the energy flow to attain a state of balance. Popular modalities include *shiatsu,* based on Chinese medicine; *amma,* a combination of East and West healing traditions; *Jin Shin Do,* utilizing oriental acupuncture and acupressure along with Taoist principles; Thai massage, blending Hindu and Chinese energy systems theory with techniques similar to *shiatsu;* and *tui na,* based on Chinese medicine and the traditional Japanese massage *amma.*

POLARITY THERAPY Polarity therapy is based on the universal principles of energy: attraction, repulsion, and neutrality. The interrelation of these principles forms the basis for every aspect of life, including our experience of health, wellness, and disease. With this understanding, polarity therapy addresses the interdependence of body, mind, and spirit; the importance of relationships; and the value of creating a way of life in harmony with nature.

PRENATAL/PREGNANCY MASSAGE Many methods of massage therapies are effective and safe prenatally and during the labor and postpartum periods of women's pregnancies. Prenatally, specific techniques can reduce the discomforts and concerns of pregnancy and enhance the physiological and emotional well-being of both mother and fetus. Skilled touch facilitates labor, shortening labor times and easing pain and anxiety. In the postpartum period, specialized techniques rebalance structure, physiology, and emotions of the new mother, and may help her to bond with and care for her infant.

REIKI Buddhist in nature, Reiki (pronounced "ray-key") is the combining of universal energy with individual energy to open pathways of healing. It teaches that disease is not separate from the body; it is the body out of balance. Rediscovered by the Japanese scholar of theology, Mikao Usui, around 1921, this energy healing method involves placing the hands on or just above the body in order to align chakras and bring healing energy to organs and glands. The practitioner, trained to access and serve as a channel for the life energy, uses a passive touch that some recipients experience as warmth or tingling. The hands remain in position for three to five minutes, sequentially covering ten to twelve positions over the body. Treatments work by dissolving or eliminating toxic energy and substances from many levels of one's being, whether physical, emotional, or mental. This works to strengthen the harmonic flow of energy within the body.

SPORTS MASSAGE Sports massage consists of specific components designed to reduce injury, alleviate inflammation, provide warm-up and so forth. It works for amateur and professional athletes before, during, and after competition, and within their training regimens.

SWEDISH MASSAGE One of the most well-known massage techniques, Swedish massage is a vigorous system of treatment designed to energize the body by stimulating circulation. Five basic strokes, all flowing toward the heart, are used to manipulate the soft tissues of the body. The disrobed recipient is covered by a sheet, with only the area being worked on exposed. Practitioners use a combination of kneading, rolling, vibrational, percussive, and tapping movements, with application of oil to reduce friction on the skin. The many benefits of Swedish massage may include generalized relaxation; dissolution of scar tissue adhesions; and improved circulation, which may speed healing and reduce swelling from injury.

STONE THERAPY Stones of all shapes, sizes, and temperatures (ranging from 0 to 130 degrees) are used during stone massage to elicit physical healing, mental relaxation, and a spiritual connection to earth energy. Warm stones in massage encourage the exchange of blood and lymph, and provide soothing heat for deep-tissue work. Cold stones aid with inflammation, moving blood out of the area, and balancing inner energies. Stones are placed in various positions on the body and may also be used in stroking to warm the surface anatomy.

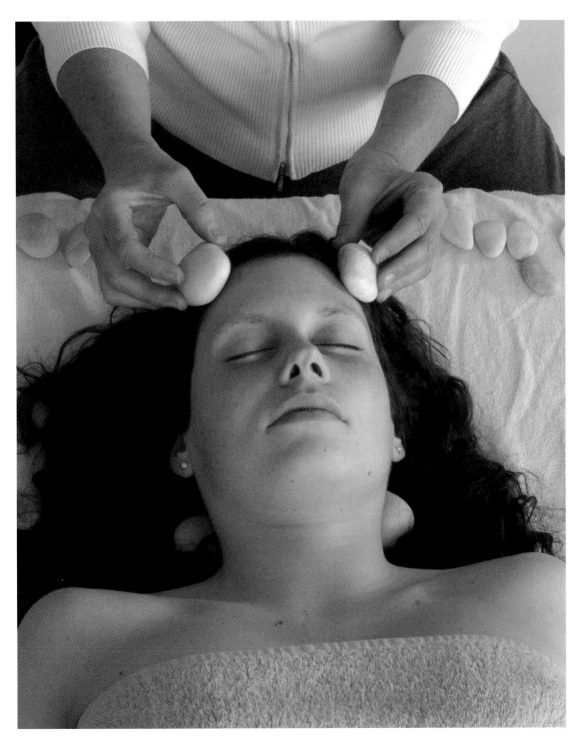

CHAPTER ELEVEN

HEALING STONE MASSAGE: AN EARTH REMEDY FOR OUR TIMES

If you want inner peace
Find it in solitude, not speed.
And if you would find yourself,
Look to the land from which you came
And to which you will one day go.
—STEWART UDALL

IN THIS CHAPTER you will learn ways to naturally incorporate warmed stones into a massage session even if you are untrained in professional massage therapy. Before you give a stone massage, relax and allow your intuition to guide you. Try one of the meditations in chapter 2, or the exercise "Bridging Heaven and Earth." Have fun selecting different stone shapes and textures. Massage friends and family with them, using your favorite oil or aromatherapy blend. Warmed stones naturally go with aromatherapy and essential oils, as well as with crystals and chakra-balancing gemstones. Above all, remember that the warmed stones are extensions of your own hands and as such are expressions of the joy in your heart.

Of course, for safety's sake you will want to balance your intuition with science and also take common sense precautions. Because you will be working with heat, the following sections on thermotherapy and massage show you how to be careful and well-informed so that you will have the necessary confidence to give a beneficial stone massage.

You might wish to start off with a stone massage for deep relaxation, and then progress later to a more lively sequence for the athlete in your life. Or, it

Stone massage is especially effective when given in an atmosphere of tranquility

may be interesting to try a simple cold stone application to relieve your own headache, which may be due to tension or sinus pressure. Another way to work with healing stones is to combine the warm and the cool stones with crystals for polarity balancing. The possibilities are truly endless!

BEFORE YOU GIVE A STONE MASSAGE

In order to best determine whether or not a certain therapy or healing modality is appropriate, we must first understand the body's basic anatomy and physiology, or its basic systems and their properties. A complete study of all of these systems is beyond the scope of this book, but there are a number of points of particular relevance to massage and thermotherapy. These involve the cellular, musculoskeletal, fluid, and organ systems

THE CELLULAR SYSTEM To begin the exploration into the body's systems, we will look at the cellular level. The cells are the matrix from which all states and processes evolve. A cell's basic structure comprises an outer semi-permeable membrane that encloses a jelly-like fluid called cytoplasm, which is seventy to eighty percent water.

THE FLUID SYSTEM Next are the fluid systems of the body, which have a composition very similar to that of the ocean. In fact, our fluids have one internal oceanic source: the interstitial fluid. Composed of collagen fiber bundles, tiny proteoglycan filaments, and water, the interstitium is a gel-like medium surrounding all of the cells and giving tissue its tensionlerength. The interstitial fluid, though gel-like, is the transport medium throughout the entire body for nutrients and oxygen. It crosses thin membranes and changes into blood, lymph, cellular fluid, cerebrospinal fluid and synovial joint fluid.

Water is one of the simplest compounds found on earth, and nearly eighty percent of our bodies is composed of it. It is the solvent that cleanses our organ system, the radiator that absorbs warmth and maintains it evenly, and our coolant too—all at the same time.

The water molecule is a very strong one, with one oxygen atom bonded to two hydrogen atoms. Electrically, water molecules are called "dipole" molecules, because one side is slightly positively charged, and the other is negatively charged. This makes the action of the water molecule similar to that of a magnet!

In other words, its positive side will be attracted to, or will attract, particles having a negative charge, and likewise its negative side will be attracted to positively charged particles. This action becomes important when the fluids of the body, which are mostly water, come into direct or indirect contact with the numerous compounds whose elements are held together not by covalent bonds, but by geomagnetic and electromagnetic charges—compounds such as stones. The chemistry of the bloodstream is affected by the combined influence of stones and the increased circulation of fluid.

THE CIRCULATORY SYSTEM When one water molecule comes into contact with two atoms held together by the geomagnetic force present in stone, it will, because water is a dipole, cancel some of the electrical attraction between the two atoms. This creates a change in the ionic matrix of the internal fluidic environment. As some of the attraction is cancelled, the two atoms will move further apart, and more water molecules will flow in. Finally the initial attraction between the atoms (stone and water, or water and toxins in the bloodstream) is eliminated, and the atoms are separated by more flowing water.

The "compound" has thus been partly or wholly dissolved by the water, and its flow increased. In addition, the water acts as a conductor of the geomagnetic force in the stone, enabling it to influence the body.

ORGAN AND GLAND SYSTEMS The organ and gland systems of the body make up the inner content, the core body. When attention is drawn into the core of the body, the parasympathetic part of the nervous system is stimulated. This is the part of the nervous system that slows things down and supports the processes of digestion, assimilation, and elimination. During stone massage with the belly stone layout, the recipient will become more conscious of the core body, and you will see the breathing deepen and relax. This is a sign that the parasympathetic aspect of the nervous system is balancing the action of the sympathetic nervous system, which is the "fight or flight" responder.

The benefit of any massage dramatically increases with the intention of your touch, the full presence of your being. In a way this is more important than how skilled the application and how advanced your techniques may be.

THERMOTHERAPY PRINCIPLES

Healing stone massage integrates thermotherapy with basic relaxation massage strokes.

It includes warm and hot stones—sometimes in alternation with cold stones—placed directly on the body in conjunction with relaxation massage. Localized heat produces vasodilation and increased circulation of fluids into the area of focus. Edgar Cayce, the healer and prophet, recommended thermotherapy in the form of hot castor oil compresses. Applied locally over liver, stomach, and colon, these compresses help to dissolve masses, adhesions and congestion in the organs. Scientific research supports his findings that prolonged application (forty to sixty minutes per treatment) of heat over an organ produces a local sauna effect. Venous dilation and reduction in adhesive tissue or mass occurs. Increased circulation enhances the delivery of oxygen and nutrients to the organs and nerve cells. When the heat comes from a stone instead of an electric heating pad, there are the added benefits of polarity balancing and geomagnetism.

In addition to warm stone massage, there will be times that you might want to use cold stones to reduce pain and swelling. The application of contrasting cool or iced stone temperatures to target areas like joints and inflamed muscles produces a vascular flushing, pumping, and draining action. This is the result of rapid contraction following dilation. The pumping of fresh fluids through joint spaces and muscle tissue stimulates movement of fluids and tissues that are otherwise inaccessible to the touch, such as the bursa; it also

OPPOSITE: **Combining hot and cool stones can have great therapeutic benefits**

drains metabolic waste from muscle spindles following exertion. This, in combination with cleansing massage strokes or more specific deep tissue massage, greatly benefits your work.

Stone massage also works the surface anatomy with heated stones. The stones used in the hands for active massage stroking are hotter than the warm layout stones. They prepare the soft tissue for your more focused attention.

EARTH MEDICINE PRINCIPLES IN STONE THERAPY

Stones are natural permanent magnets. Their healing potential has been recognized for millennia.

Traditional medicine tells us that the elements of nature are expressed physically and emotionally in the human experience. The principles of Five Element medicine consider health and disease to be a continuum and a process, rather than a static diagnosis. For example, elements of air and ether are manifested physically in the human body by dryness, coldness, lightness, changeableness, versatility, subtlety, brittleness and refinement; the fire element by heat, action, intensity, passion, and acuity; the earth element by solidity, heaviness, smoothness, softness, coldness, stability, and oiliness.

In accordance with traditional medicine, the better one understands the innate strengths and weaknesses of the person you are trying to help, the more effective massage with heat or other adjuncts will be. Don't worry; if the person you are working with can tolerate a warm bath or shower, he or she can safely enjoy warm stone massage.

The development of disease or imbalance manifests as the result of "accumulation of excess." The "accumulation of excess" will present varying symptom patterns listed below.

SYMPTOMS OF ELEMENTS IN EXCESS

AIR & ETHER	FIRE & WATER	EARTH & WATER
Emaciation	Fever	Chronic depression
Constipation	Inflammation	Heaviness
Coldness	Hunger	Lethargy
Dizziness	Thirst	Excess sleep
Insomnia	Insomnia	Productive cough
Confusion	Burning sensations	Respiratory problems
Depression	Anger	Edema
Fear	Skin eruptions	Sluggish digestion
Doubt	Yellowness in skin or eyes	Weight gain
Insecurity	Pride	Attachment/Greed
Pallor or grayness in skin tone	Egotism	
Dry skin	Arrogance	
Chills	Nausea	

The principles of earth medicine are based on the concept "like increases (or aggravates) like." For instance, to treat an Air and Ether type body, or for treatments in the autumn, which is a cool, windy season, you would give warming, nourishing treatments. You would want to make sure that your massage uses plenty of oil, because heat alone can dry out the already dry system, further aggravating the drying nature of air.

FACTORS TO CONSIDER

TIME OF YEAR

Air and Ether are aggravated in cold, dry, windy, late autumn
Fire is aggravated in hot summer and early fall
Earth and Water are aggravated in cold, damp winter

TIME OF LIFE

Water and Earth are dominant between birth and sixteen years of age
Fire is dominant between sixteen and forty-five years of age
Air and Ether are dominant between forty-five years of age to the end of life

7 Elemental Weaknesses and Natural Therapies

ELEMENTAL WEAKNESS	GOVERNING PLANET	MERIDIAN/GLAND	NATURAL STONE THERAPY
Excess heat	Sun	Small intestine Heart Pineal	Cooling therapies (Salty foods) Moonstones Light strokes
Excess coldness	Moon	Triple warmer Pericardium Thymus	Warming therapies (Pungent foods) Warm layout stones
Excess heaviness or dampness	Jupiter	Conception vessel	Lightening therapies Contrast: hot/cold stones Textured stones
Excess dryness	Saturn	Stomach Spleen	Oilation therapies Warm oiled stones Deeper massage
Excess lightness	Mars	Gall bladder Governing vessel Adrenals/Pancreas	Nourishing therapies Warm stones Cool stones Deep massage therapy
Excess oiliness	Venus	Bladder Kidney Thyroid	Drying therapies using clays and clay baths
Mixed types of imbalances	Mercury/Nodes of the moon	Pituitary gland	Warming Nourishing therapies Warm/hot stone massage therapy

COOLING MASSAGE THERAPIES
FOR REDUCING EXCESS HEAT & LIGHTNESS IN THE BODY

USE THESE OILS	AROMAS	PRESSURE	ALSO
Coconut oil	Rose and florals	Deep and sedating	Ice
Pumpkin seed oil	Coriander	Precise	Cool stones
Sunflower oil	Sandalwood		

WARMING AND NOURISHING MASSAGE THERAPIES
FOR REDUCING EXCESS COLDNESS AND DRYNESS IN THE BODY

USE THESE OILS	AROMAS	PRESSURE	ALSO
Olive oil	Rose/Jasmine	Soothing	Warm stones
Beeswax	Orange	Slow	Warm compress
Almond oil	Camphor	Sedating	Ginger compress
Sesame oil	Ginger		Castor oil pack
			Dry brushing

REDUCING/STIMULATING MASSAGE THERAPIES
FOR REDUCING EXCESS HEAVINESS AND OILINESS/DAMPNESS IN THE BODY

USE OILS	AROMAS	PRESSURE	ALSO
Sparingly	Eucalyptus	Vigorous	Hot and cold stones
	Citrus	Deep	Percussion
	Grapefruit	Penetrating	Dry brushing
	Mint		

SPECIFIC CONSTITUTIONAL CONSIDERATIONS IN STONE MASSAGE:

FOR BALANCING OR REDUCING AIR AND ETHER (DRYNESS). Keep your strokes long, smooth, steady, and very slow. You want your stones to provide a steadying effect and not become another *thing* that the recipient must think about.

Use plenty of warmed oil, especially sesame, jojoba and beeswax blends. Use hot stones in long strokes along the long bones. Circle the joints with hot stones and oils. Do not tap stones or move too quickly. Focus on abdominal massage with warm oiled stones. Use castor oil on the feet and belly. Work from the feet inward to the core body. Apply a warm brow stone, and cover the eyes with a slightly warmed eye pillow filled with flax seeds. Use warming and relaxing aromatherapy essences, such as lavender, tangerine, rose, cedarwood, or ginger.

FOR BALANCING OR REDUCING FIRE (HEAT AND LIGHTNESS). Deepen your strokes, and use more precision. Apply a cool moonstone to the brow, and do not use an eye pillow over the eyes. Try a cool eye pad instead, or cucumber slices with two small cold moonstones on top. Enliven the strokes and incorporate more petrissage (kneading), wringing, and pointwork. Start at the head and move downward to the feet. Use floral aromas such as ylang ylang, rose, and jasmine, and also the *pitta*-pacifying sandalwood, chamomile, and coconut oils. Follow the Moonstone Facial instructions after the basic warm stone massage (see below).

FOR BALANCING OR REDUCING FIRE AND EXCESS EARTH AND WATER (DAMPNESS AND HEAVINESS). Use textured stones, with more vigor in active strokes. Try

adding some sea salt and/or rosemary oil to your base cream or oil, and massage with warm stones. Circle the joints with heat. Apply the "waterfall" strokes, alternating iced and hot temperatures. Keep the body warm with layout stones. Don't use a brow stone or eye pillow over eyes, as too much "grounding" for these types of people can produce mental depression. Stay alert and laugh with your recipient.

The idea is to make sure your remedies do not cause another imbalance more serious than the original one.

GEOMAGNETISM AND PRINCIPLES OF PHYSICS IN HEALING

Since the emergence of human consciousness, healers and mystics have revered the power of natural "forces" to heal. The question we may ask ourselves when using stones of any sort in massage or healing is "how are these forces transmitted?"

From physics, we know that a *force* between two particles is transmitted by the continual exchange of *opposite, attractive electrical charges*. Every particle on earth, including those found in stones, is composed of electromagnetically charged ions. Every particle also possesses either a positive charge or a negative charge. Every electromagnetically charged particle also continually emits and reabsorbs virtual photons—light—and/or exchanges them with other charged particles.

For example, when two electrons (two particles with a negative ionic charge) meet one another, they are repelled. The same thing occurs when two protons meet (two particles with a positive ionic charge). They repel one another. But, when one proton and one electron meet, they attract and exchange virtual photons, or light.

The force within the stone simply and gently completes the exchange of virtual photons with those in the human energy field, which is also electromagnetically animated, or charged. This photon exchange cancels, or brings to neutrality, the electromagnetic energy field permeating the physical body. It is experienced by the subtle system first. The nerves and brain find a calm alertness. From these pathways of cognition, the rest of the body reorganizes and settles internally.

WESTERN MEDICINE PRINCIPLES OF STONE MASSAGE

BENEFITS OF HEALING STONE MASSAGE

Here is a list of the known benefits of stone massage to the basic body systems, according to Western orthopedic medicine.

MUSCULOSKELETAL SYSTEM

1. *softens and releases connective tissue*

2. *reduces muscle fibrosity and tightness*

3. *increases range of motion in joints*

VASCULAR SYSTEM

1. *improves circulation to extremities*

2. *increases rate, amplitude and excursion of blood circulation*

NERVOUS SYSTEM

1. *sedates central nervous system*

2. *shifts "stress" perspective by balancing parasympathetic and sympathetic systems*

3. *decreases irritability as increased blood flow nourishes nerve cells*

LYMPHATIC FLUID SYSTEM

1. promotes lymph drainage and cleansing

2. detoxifies with the solvent action of water; facilitates cell hydration and flushing

VISCERAL/ORGAN SYSTEM

1. decongests liver by relaxing ducts

2. relaxes colon

3. detoxifies blood with sweating

SPECIAL BENEFITS OF PRENATAL WARM STONE MASSAGE

- relaxation and decreased insomnia; physical and emotional relaxation; reduction of the fatigue that is so common in pregnancy; emotional support through nurturing touch

- greater circulation; improvement in the baby's oxygen supply; help with preventing varicose veins and swelling

- stress relief on weight-bearing joints such as ankles, lower back, and pelvis; relief from muscle pain and joint stiffness; mother is enabled to begin labor with less tension in back, pelvis, and legs

- greater acceptance of the beauty, healthiness, and power of pregnancy; confidence in body image is boosted

- faster recovery of energy and muscle tone after the birth; reduction of postpartum stress

- reduction of calf cramping; headache and sinus congestion relief

PRECAUTIONS

Thermotherapy and stone massage involve the use of extreme temperatures (hot as well as cold) and also incorporate deep pressure massage. Therefore it is wise to take care and observe the following precautions.

Avoid any areas where there are abnormalities or swelling of the skin or underlying tissues; broken skin or open wounds; rashes, including athlete's foot and impetigo; lesions; sunburn; or boils including conjunctivitis.

Herpes (cold sores) and post-herpetic neuralgia should not be treated with heat.

For cardiac patients or individuals with a history of heart or blood vessel disease, use caution and moderate temperatures.

PRECAUTIONS FOR PREGNANCY

In order to give stone massage safely, when working with pregnant women, it is important to

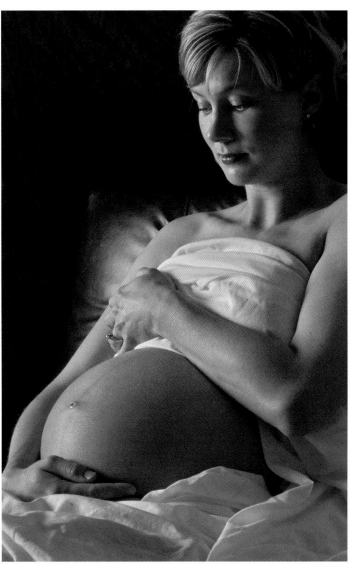

understand what is happening in their bodies during this time. Warm stone massage may be contraindicated in a very few cases, or there may be cautions and restrictions to take into consideration. Abdominal massage is contraindicated during pregnancy. Warm and hot stones must not be applied in the area of the belly. A few light strokes, passive touch, and some forms of energy work may be performed safely. Direct and sustained pressure during prenatal stone massage should not be applied to the area between the ankle bone and heel. This area is considered by many massage practitioners and reflexologists to relate to the uterus and vagina, and it is thought that heavy pressure to this area could promote early labor. Assuming there are no other precautions or considerations, it should be all right to massage the rest of the feet. Hot stone massage is effective for many conditions, but should be moderated in pregnancy by using warm stones only. The warm stone therapy should be limited to twenty minutes in the second and third trimesters of pregnancy. Below is a general list of contraindications for pre-natal stone massage.

- *Morning sickness, nausea or vomiting*
- *Vaginal bleeding or discharge*
- *Diabetes*
- *Contagious illness*
- *Any malignant condition*
- *Fever*
- *Decrease in fetal movements for twenty-four hours*
- *Diarrhea*
- *High blood pressure*
- *Pain in abdomen or pre-eclampsia*
- *Excessive swelling*
- *A meal immediately before the massage*
- *Local contraindications such as a bruise or wound, etc.*

GENERAL CONTRAINDICATIONS

Do not perform *hot* stone massage if the recipient

- *Feels nauseated*
- *Is in severe pain*

- *Has a fever*

- *Has local contraindications*

- *Has lymphangitis (inflammation of the lymphatic vessels)*

- *Has swollen glands (draining the glands may cause an infection to spread)*

- *Has had whiplash or other acute trauma within the last forty-eight hours; apply cold stones or ice to reduce bleeding into tissues*

- *Has rheumatoid arthritis; avoid heated stones over acutely inflamed joints*

EQUIPMENT AND MATERIALS YOU WILL NEED

The following is a list of the equipment essential to performing stone massage.

- *Assorted massage stones: a variety of sizes, contours, and textures*

- *Massage table*

- *Stone warmer appliance*

- *Bolsters or props*

- *Sponge and liquid detergent for washing stones*

- *Natural antiseptic water treatment*

- *Cold water dipping bowl*

GETTING STARTED

HOW TO WARM YOUR MASSAGE STONES

For warming massage stones an electric skillet is recommended instead of a crock pot or large turkey roaster. Electric skillets are easily controllable, very efficient, easy to clean, and quite safe for heating stones for massage. They make your work simple and hygienic because you will be able to use fresh clean water for each session.

Cleaning the warmer in between sessions is also simple. All you need to do is unplug and empty it, and then refill it with clean water. It takes only seven to ten minutes to bring the stones' temperatures up to the desired range. Electric skillets or frying appliances are available at most general department or discount stores, in the housewares section. A large skillet is approximately fifteen inches across and is oblong or round.

Selecting your massage stones from a skillet is easy because it is shallow in comparison to larger, deeper eighteen-quart turkey roasters or crock pots. Immersion into warm water will warm your stones. It is not the quantity of water that affects the temperature of the stones. In fact, even a dry skillet may be used to warm stones; in this case, however, reheating stones will take longer than immersion in water.

You can fit approximately forty-two stones, ranging in size from small facial and toe stones (1"-2" each) to large belly and body-sized stones (3"-7" diameter), in one 15" electric skillet.

METHOD FOR WARMING STONES IN AN ELECTRIC SKILLET

You will just need one large unit, fifteen or sixteen inches across. First warm the stones to be used in foundation layouts. Once the warm stones are in place on your recipient and on the massage table, you can increase the heat in the skillet for the active working stones. These will be re-used frequently during the session.

Turn the skillet on to "WARM." This is the lowest setting, often just below "SIMMER." If you are using a thermometer, this setting is around 115-120 degrees.

1. PLACE FIFTEEN "FOUNDATION" STONES INTO YOUR WARMER, SIDE BY SIDE

You'll be able to get all fifteen foundation stones into a 15" electric skillet if they are placed side by side rather than flat along the bottom surface of the unit. These stones are to be just *warm*, not hot.

The foundation stones are as follows.

- *2 trapezius inserts*

- *I neck stone*

- *2 belly-organ stones*

- *2 hand rests*

- *I heart stone*

- *6 spinal layout stones*

- *I sacrum stone*

Do not add any other stones to the warmer YET.

2. FILL WARMER TO THE BRIM WITH WATER.

3. THE LID IS NOT NEEDED DURING A SESSION.

4. ADD YOUR CHOICE OF NATURAL ANTIBACTERIAL AGENT FROM THE LIST:

- *15 drops of lavender essential oil*

- *15 drops grapefruit seed extract*

- *10 drops of tea tree oil*

5. TURN ON SKILLET TO WARM (115-120 DEGREES). WAIT FIVE TO SEVEN MINUTES.

6. ROTATE EACH STONE. REPEAT AS NEEDED UNTIL ALL STONES ARE WARM.

7. ADD YOUR EIGHT TOE AND SEVEN FACIAL STONES, KEEPING THEM IN TWO SEPARATE CORNERS SO THAT THEY ARE EASIER TO RETRIEVE.

Wait until all stones feel comfortable and warm to the touch, about 10 minutes. They should be as warm as a hot bath. Now ask the recipient to sit up while you place three pairs of spinal layout stones, plus a sacrum stone if you like, on the massage table. You will be surprised at how much the padding of the massage table absorbs the bumpiness of the stones. The recipient should feel completely comfortable lying on the stones.

8. ONCE ALL STONES ARE IN USE ON THE TABLE, TURN UP THE HEAT IN THE WARMER BY TWO NOTCHES TO HOT, OR 125–130 DEGREES. ADD YOUR REMAINING STONES; THESE ARE YOUR PALM STONES.

These are the stones with which you will give the massage. They should fit comfortably in your hand and be of a variety of sizes and shapes for different techniques we will explore later.

STONE TEMPERATURE CONTROL AND GUIDELINES

Your water temperature can be controlled in a matter of seconds mid-session by adjusting the temperature-control dial up or down one increment as needed. The water temperature will change in a few minutes. This makes it easy to regulate the stones' temperature. Microwave ovens are never recommended for heating stones because of the iron and other ores they contain.

Although it may seem logical to aim for a certain numeric degree on a thermometer, you ought to rely on the common sense "touch test." If a stone is too hot to touch, it will be too hot to apply to your recipient's skin. Likewise there is no reason to use thermometers, gloves, or tongs in your stone therapy work. Take into account the fact that no two people are alike; so you must

communicate, watching the response to stone temperature at all times. Your recipient may like a hot stone (130 degrees) on his or her shoulders, but may prefer warm (115 degrees) on the abdomen.

SAFETY PRECAUTIONS

Wearing gloves and using tongs prevents you from directly experiencing the temperature of the stone. This is unsafe. Relying in session upon thermometers or the appliance's standard numeric temperature settings to gauge stone temperatures is not a safe practice. Indeed, once a session is underway and stones are removed from and added to the warmer, a true temperature reading for an individual stone is impossible. If you work with stones that possess high iron ore content, once they are warmed through to their core you will not need to reheat them mid-session anyway. This is another practical and safety reason to work with high-grade stones.

Be sure that your recipient holds the "test" stone in place on his or her forearm for a minimum of ten seconds. That is how long it takes to feel the true temperature of the stone from the core, rather than only from the surface.

CARE AND MAINTENANCE OF HEALING STONES

It does not require much time to clean your stones between uses. Wash them well with warm water and soap. Try alcohol to remove oil and lotion from the surface.

Certain aspects of hygiene are non-negotiable, such as washing the stones and changing the water for each person. Your cleanup will progress quickly if you focus more on the oily stones and less on the dry layout stones.

After having cleaned them thoroughly, the best way to store your stones is in a well-ventilated space, preferably with exposure to fresh air.

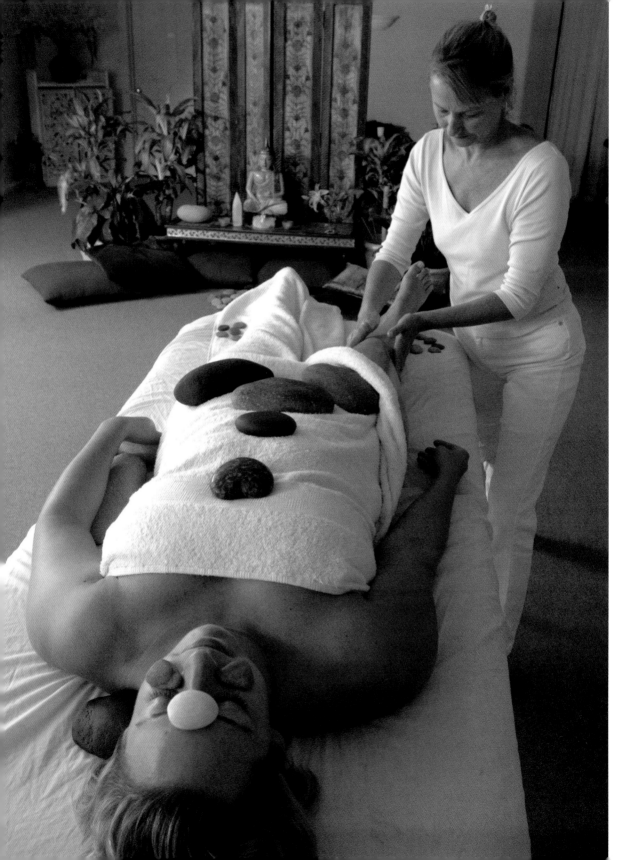

CHAPTER TWELVE

THE PRACTICE OF HEALING STONE MASSAGE

EARTH AND STONE HEALING PRINCIPLES

HEALING STONE MASSAGE is an energy-based approach to massage. Therefore, a working knowledge of the energy centers as well as the organ systems will help you determine which layouts, techniques, stones, and temperatures to use. For example, when a meridian point or chakra is congested it will feel hot, hard, or puffy. When it is depleted, it will feel cold, hollow, or empty. If energy is depleted, you can tonify or strengthen it by massaging with hot or warm stones.

When you sense that an area is weak or low in energy, and you rub a warmed stone lightly over it, maintain evenness of pressure, much like drawing a bead under a blanket. In a short time you will be able to feel energy moving in the tissues as the stone activates the area. It isn't necessary to exert very heavy pressure with a stone over an energy line or chakra. The matrix of the energy system is subtle and refined and may be affected at a deep level with just a light application.

Since we are using non-specific beach or river stones instead of crystals, it is perfectly safe to use just one type of stone. Sometimes healers working with crystals and gemstones caution against using only one type of stone for every placement over the chakras; they understand that some people are unable to handle such an infusion of strong current. Likewise, it is safe to use all black, all grey or just mixed colors of warm non-specific river or beach stones. Again, if we were using crystals or gemstones, we would avoid using all black stones for the chakras, because the grounding potential of black crystals might have a depressing effect. However, a closer look at the internal composition of apparently black sea stones reveals many minerals and a full spectrum of color rays.

These stones should not be placed over clothing; instead, they should be applied directly on the body. You can see here some ideas for placements.

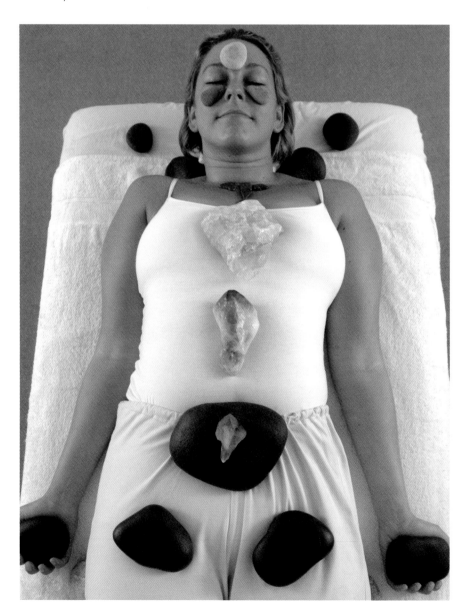

Here are some correspondences to the chakras for your stone layouts. When we speak about layouts we are referring to either warm or cold stones placed over or under the body. These placements allow the energy in the stones to assist the body's energy to flow naturally from the root to the crown.

FIRST AND SECOND CHAKRAS (NOT FOR PREGNANT WOMEN)

- *Applied to the front of the body, the layout relaxes muscles and ligament attachments in the pelvis, and relieves cramps.*

- *Positioned under the lower back, it relaxes muscles and ligament attachments and reduces hip and lower back pain.*

- *Kidneys and adrenals have a special affinity for warmth. Apply stone layout to back while recipient is lying face-up, and again when face down. Do not use cold stones over this region.*

- *Stone layouts applied to the first and second chakras ground and stabilize awareness in the present moment.*

THIRD CHAKRA

- *Stones applied to the belly and/or solar plexus before a meal will tonify digestion, increasing metabolism and enzyme production.*

- *Alternating hot and cold stones with abdominal massage will amplify the tonifying effect on chronic blockages in the abdomen.*

- *Wait thirty minutes before giving an abdominal massage to someone who has just eaten.*

- *Use one or two large warm stones over the liver region, with castor oil, to produce a compress. The softening properties of castor oil are known to reduce adhesions; increase nourishing blood flow to the ducts; and move stagnant liver energy, allowing for toxins to pass and for cellular rejuvenation.*

- *A stone layout applied to the third chakra realigns the individual will with the spirit, and promotes receptivity and centering for the emotions.*

FOURTH AND FIFTH CHAKRAS

• *For lung decongestion, place warmed stones under the upper back.*

• *Warm stones relax bronchial respiration, giving possible relief for asthma. Do not apply too much weight over the lungs of asthmatic people or those prone to anxiety.*

• *For emotional problems, use a room-temperature rose quartz instead of a heated stone on the front of the body directly over the heart, with the warmed stones under the upper back. This layout helps to calm emotions.*

• *The heart is one of the sites of the fire element in the body and can be aggravated when too much heat is added in healing. Keep the temperature of the stone over the heart at body temperature, not hot.*

• *Two warm stones under the shoulders and one small warm stone under the neck relieve chronic neck tension.*

• *For headache, use cool stones under the neck. The root of the tongue and the throat chakra soften. They direct an "inner smile" to the rest of the body.*

SIXTH AND SEVENTH CHAKRAS

• *Place a small warm stone over the brow between the two eyebrows to center a busy mind.*

• *Place a small cool stone over the brow between the two eyebrows to reduce irritability and impatience.*

• *Use aromatherapy such as rose, sandalwood, or your favorite scent to support a meditative feeling.*

OPPOSITE: **Preparing to lie on the foundation layout.**

154

CENTRAL CHANNEL

Prolonged application of warm stones to the spine calms the central nervous system. It communicates a slower vibratory rate to every nerve pathway and chakra center, affecting the entire organism. The warm stones may be placed underneath the body or over the body, as shown here.

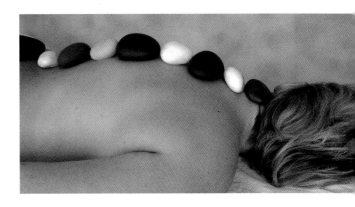

There are important yet subtle differences between lying over stones, having stones laid over the body, or being actively massaged with stones. When you lie over warm stones, you impose your own body weight on or impress yourself into the properties of the stones. When you have stones laid upon your body, you are receiving these properties in a more passive manner. Many people prefer the feeling of lying over stones, citing the deeper contact and delivery.

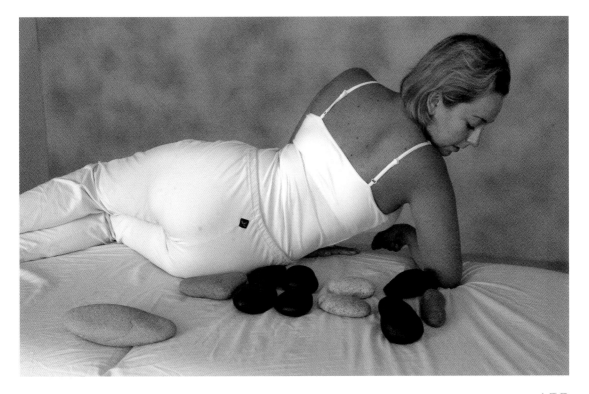

THE HEALING STONE MASSAGE SEQUENCE

The basic healing stone massage in this chapter will show you how to create a holistic energy-balancing stone massage sequence. After some practice, you may decide to change the patterns and the placements. We will begin with warm stones underneath the body. These are called foundation stones.

Have your recipient sit up while warm foundation stones are laid out along the midline of table. These should be warm, not hot.

TIP: Select two or three pairs of matching flat oval stones, using the flattest stones for the broad thoracic region and a larger, more plump pair under the natural lumbar curve.

Adjust the neck and trapezius stones for comfort.

Insert the handrest stones outside of the towel, not on top of it.

Place either one warm or one cool stone on the brow.

Place a pillow or bolster under the knees.

Next, after all the foundation stones are in place, turn the dial of your warmer up to the active working temperature. This is hotter than for the layout stones, but it is not important to use a thermometer. As long as you can handle the stones, and you utilize the common-sense touch test, the temperature is safe. Communication is vital during a stone massage.

START THE STONE MASSAGE

When you first begin to massage with stones, it may feel awkward, and you may tend to grip the stones. Allow the stones to become an extension of your relaxed body and hands instead. Pay attention to your own comfort, and pause to breathe deeply and slowly if you feel anxious at all. Your anxiety should soon change to a more playful feeling.

I. Adjust the pillows and stones for comfort. Get feedback often.

2. Start the massage at the feet. Use warm massage oil in cold weather. In warm weather, use massage oil or lotion with a few drops of peppermint or basil essential oils added.

3. Apply massage oil or cream to the legs with long flowing effleurage strokes.

ABOVE: **Step 2**
LEFT: **Step 4**

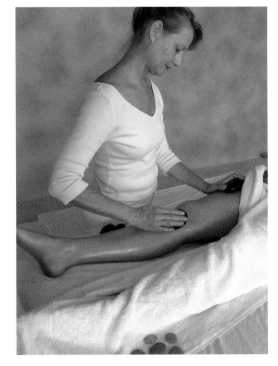

4. Use hot round or oval stones to massage the legs. Flip your stones and replace them frequently enough to maintain even heat. Follow with deeper massage by "edging" and "striping" into the muscles with your stones. Alternate these techniques with "ironing," using the broad, flat sides of your stones. Try adding some deep compressions into the belly of the muscles next. This is done by placing flat stones under your hand and exerting an abrupt pumping move with direct pressure, as if to flatten the muscle against the bone. This will spread the muscle fibers and allow them to receive more incoming blood flow. This is especially cleansing to the large muscles of the thigh.

BELOW: **Step 4**

5. End the foot and leg sequence with more foot massage. Be mindful of delicate bony points around the ankles, keeping lighter pressure in general on these points. Insert a warm stone into the spaces between each toe. Cover the feet and legs with a towel when you are finished.

6. Apply massage cream to the recipient's hands and arms using effleurage strokes.

7. Use small hot round stones to massage the arms upward, toward the torso. Flip and replace the stones often. Follow with deeper arm massage by "edging" and "striping" into the muscles with your stones. Alternate these techniques with "ironing," using the broad, flat sides of your stones along the muscles of the forearm. Try adding some focused stone massage to the wrists and hands, including the fingers. If the handrest stone has cooled from exposure to the air, remember to reheat it before placing your recipient's hand back down over it.

BELOW: **Step 5**

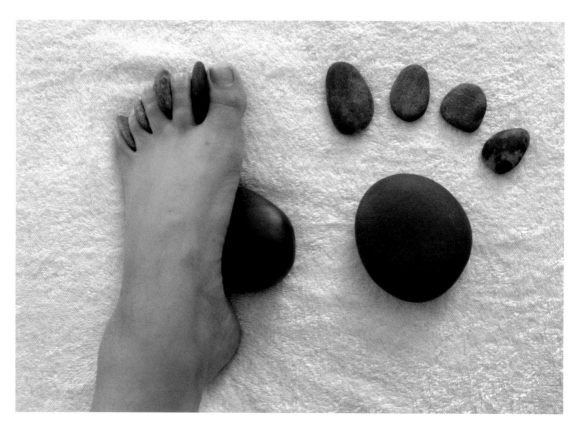

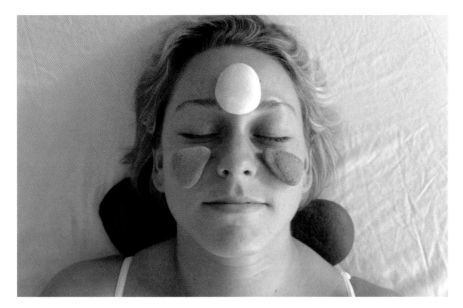

LEFT: **Step 8**

BELOW: **Step 9**

8. For the shoulders and neck, remove the shoulder and neck layout stones and use small hot stones in your hands to massage along areas of tension. Follow with deep massage with your hands only.

9. For the scalp and face remove the layout stones so there is room for your hands to move underneath, and then massage the scalp and neck. Facial stones are best if they are small, thin, and smooth—teardrop- or oval-shaped—and are used without lotion or oil. Facial stones are always applied with light pressure. To induce serenity, keep an evenness to the pace and depth. For the facial massage, there are two options. Warm stones are good for relieving sinus pressure and jaw pain; cool stones are good for relieving headache, toxicity, fatigue, and puffiness around the eyes.

COOLING MOONSTONE FACIAL; COOLING THERAPY PRINCIPLES

After you have massaged the body with the warm stones try a facial massage with cool milky quartzite for rejuvenation. The moonstone facial integrates many ancient medicine principles. It begins with cool white quartzite and marble stones. Field collection of these stones is limited; they are primarily found along the beaches of New England, India, and France. (See resources directory in the back of the book for availability.) They are not actual moonstones, which are semi-precious stones. Being milky white and somewhat translucent, these metamorphic sea stones are like the moon and as such, are the dynamic opposite of darker, heat-radiating sea stones used in the warm healing stone massage.

As we know, there are correspondences between the chakras, meridians, and glands. The cooling moonstone facial benefits primarily the pineal gland, which, according to ancient Ayurvedic teachings, is linked to the astrological ruling star (or planet). As such, it is called the governing gland. Little is known about the pineal gland except that it is involved in sleep patterns and rhythms. When there is excess heat in the energy channels, there will often be an accompanying rigidity in the neck, general stiffness, headache, eye redness, or sometimes diarrhea and fevers.

The cooling moonstone facial sequence takes approximately ten minutes from start to completion. You'll need from five to eleven cool or cold stones of milky quartzite, marble, or rose quartz.

This treatment is recommended for the following conditions.

- *Sunburn*
- *Rosacea*
- *Yellowness in the skin or whites of the eyes*
- *Tinnitus*
- *TMJ*
- *Migraines (for which, use a cold stone at the base of the neck)*
- *Hangover*
- *Stiff neck*

The Cool Moonstone Facial Sequence Step-by-Step

The pressure used in this facial protocol is extremely light. The temperature of the stones varies from cool to room-temperature; they are never applied chilled or frozen to facial skin. Avoid extreme temperatures on facial skin, which is highly vulnerable to capillary damage in response to sudden vasodilation and contraction.

BOTH: **Step 1**

1. To start, you should assemble your stones within reach at the head of the table.

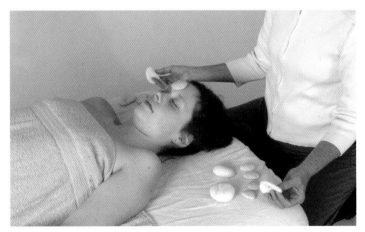

An aromatherapy adjunct for cooling protocols would be rose or sandalwood applied in a steam towel to the face, or in a diffuser in the environment. The moonstones are applied without lubrication onto clean facial skin. Place one small white stone over the brow or pineal chakra, or slightly lower over frown lines, if any. You may choose to use a moistened eye pad to cover the eyes, and place a cool stone over the pad. You may like to moisten the eye pads with rosewater.

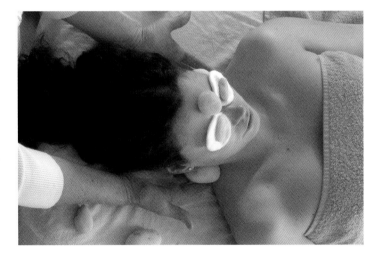

2. Press gently and hold here for five to ten seconds, anchoring awareness into the third eye point. You may slowly wind this stone three times in a counter-clockwise direction to release excess mental energies.

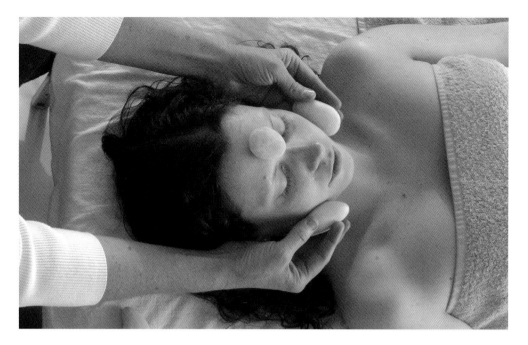

ABOVE & RIGHT:

Step 3

RIGHT: **Step 4**

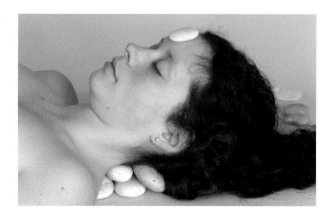

3. Next begin stroking lightly with one small moonstone in each hand, toward the lymph drainage sites located at the jawline.

4. Come up along the sides of the neck and the front of the throat. Spend approximately five minutes with this segment of the massage. Try laying cool stones along the nape of the neck.

5. Vary your strokes by adding direct sustained holds of one to three minutes each, using very light pressure, so that the cool moonstones are applied to the following points.

- *Eyelids*
- *Forehead*
- *Temples*
- *Glands*
- *Crow's feet*
- *Smile lines*
- *Chin*
- *Simultaneously to base of neck and forehead*
- *Décolletage*

It is important to move at a snail's pace, or even slower. The slower your movements, the more perceptible the sensations, and the more effective your treatment will be.

ALL: **Step 5**

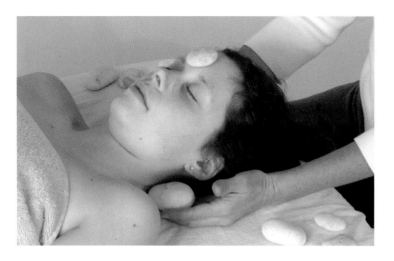

6. To conclude, remove all stones except the brow stone, and gently hold the head in both hands, cradling it for a few moments before releasing. Then go to the feet and again apply a hold, drawing the energy and consciousness back through the body and encouraging your recipient to deepen his or her breath.

ABOVE: **Step 6**

This placement is one aspect of the "waterfall technique." Contrasting thermal applications are stimulating. They have an effect similar to tapotement (percussion).

FINISHING THE STONE MASSAGE

Have your recipient turn over so you can apply massage cream to the back. Apply the lubricant in broad, spreading, effleurage strokes. For best results, include the sacral region as well as the sides of the body.

Come up over the upper shoulder and onto the upper arm. Then, starting at the lower back, massage a heart shape with your stones over the entire back. Follow this with a slow-stroke, upward-moving spinal stone massage, drawing a smaller heart over the upper back. Finally, make a third heart-shaped stroke over the mid-thoracic area.

Put the stones into the warmer as they cool down, and replace them with hotter ones.

Address the side of the body and the top of the upper shoulder. Use "raking" strokes, hand over hand, inward to the midline. Repeat this several times. Carefully introduce the edges and tips of the stones to deepen your pressure. Use contrasting stone temperatures as in the "waterfall cascade," to stimulate circulation. The alternating of warm and cold of stones in this form of thermotherapy brings a rapid exchange of blood and oxygen, and an alternating rise and fall of the respiration rate. It is a refreshing way to close your session.

164

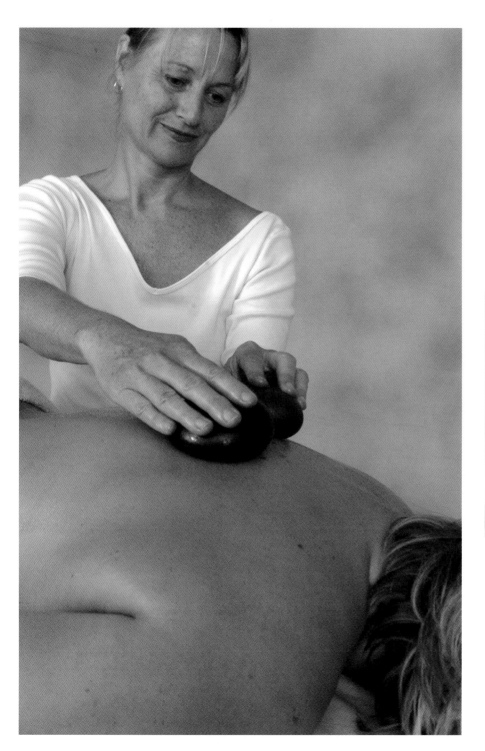

SOME CONSIDERATIONS FOR THE PREGNANCY STONE MASSAGE

In the first trimester many women will be comfortable supine or prone. Later in the pregnancy a mother-to-be may not be able to lie supine without the fetus putting pressure on the descending aorta. Such pressure can impede the flow of blood to the placenta and can also cause shortness of breath for the mother. Lying on the back may also put pressure on the inferior vena cava, resulting in feelings of lightheadedness, nausea, and backache. In short, lying prone may be difficult; though with proper bolstering it may be quite comfortable. Comfortable positions like the supine, reclining, and side-lying positions each play a role when giving massage to pregnant women.

Reclining or half-sitting may be a good alternative to lying supine. Some doctors advise against pregnant women lying on the left side while sleeping, but it is usually not a problem for the short duration of a massage.

A general principle for positioning and applying the foundation stones for prenatal massage is to fill in any spaces you find with bolsters, pillows, rolled-up towels, and warm (not hot) flat stones.

While there are no special techniques for massage during pregnancy, there are some places on the body that need special attention; the neck, chest, lower back, hips, legs, and feet.

GUIDELINES FOR MASSAGING SPECIFIC AREAS

Because of the head-forward posture of the pregnant woman, the neck and upper back may feel strained. This may also result in tension headache. The neck is most easily accessed in the supine or side-lying position. Stone massage is effective in reducing tension in the muscles of the neck and upper back. There may be trigger points to be relieved. Direct pressure to certain acupressure points can also relax neck tension.

The chest may become sunken or depressed as the pregnancy progresses. The enlarged uterus also takes up a lot of room in the abdomen, making it hard for a pregnant woman to breathe. Therefore, stone massage that frees up the rib cage and diaphragm can be important. Massage of the intercostal muscles and along the diaphragm promotes easier breathing.

Pregnancy puts pressure on the lower back. This can be addressed in the side-lying position, which in itself relieves pressure in the lower back. A simple technique to help tilt the hips back into a more normal position is a firm effleurage with the palm of the hand from the upper back to the sacrum. When your hand is over the sacrum, apply a little more pressure to help reduce discomfort in the lower back.

Childbearing puts strain on the entire lower body. The muscles of the hips and legs have to work harder to carry the added weight accumulated during pregnancy. Apply stone massage to the lower extremities as usual, ending with massage toward the heart and core body to help accumulated fluid move out of the area.

When massaging the feet, you may want to apply some gentle reflexology, avoiding pressure directly on the areas between the ankle and heel. Reflexology is safe for pregnant women; it has never been shown to have caused a body to do something it didn't want to do. Reflexology helps the body seek its own equilibrium.

FOUNDATION PROTOCOL ADAPTED FOR PREGNANCY

Do not use heavy stones, high temperatures, contrasting temperatures, or cold stones on the abdomen during pregnancy. Doing so will activate peristaltic movement and could trigger uterine contractions.

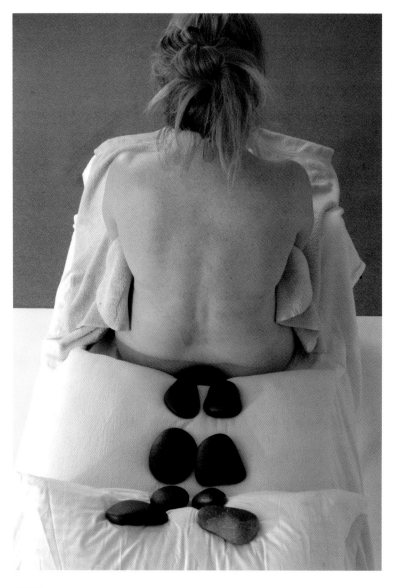

Your recipient lies face up to start, if that is comfortable. Otherwise, position her with pillows or bolsters in a semi-side-lying position.

1. Place as many warm—body-temperature only—stones as you can underneath her body, especially under her lower back and hip.

2. Place two warm stones under her shoulder blades.

3. Place one warm roll-shaped stone under her neck. Now, select a long, cylindrically-shaped warm stone to insert in the space under the neck. This stone should fit snugly and be in contact with the trapezius as well as the muscles along the side of the neck.

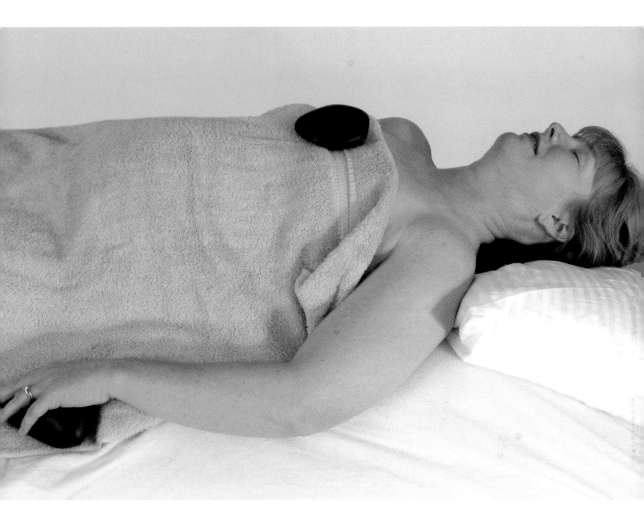

4. Place one warm handrest stone underneath, or in, each hand.

5. If the recipient is lying on her back, place one stone over the heart.

6. "Anchor" stones: The placement of anchor stones depends on the recipient's position. If she is fully supine, place a bolster under her knees and use some large warm stones under the upper thighs. This will not work in the side-lying posture.

7. Place a warm or cool stone on the brow if the recipient is lying face up.

THE MASSAGE SEQUENCE

1. Adjust pillows and stones for comfort. Get feedback often.

2. Start massaging at the feet. Use warm massage oil in cold weather, or use massage cream with a little basil oil—as an alternative to peppermint—in summer. Peppermint is not recommended during pregnancy

RIGHT: **Step 2**

BELOW: **Step 4**
OPPOSITE: **Step 5**

3. Apply massage cream to legs with effleurage strokes.

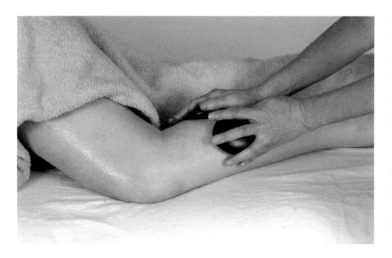

4. Use warm round stones to massage the legs. Flip your stones and replace them frequently enough to maintain even heat. Follow with deeper massage.

5. End with foot reflexology, avoiding the pregnancy points around the ankles. Keep light pressure on reflex points. Cover the legs with a towel.

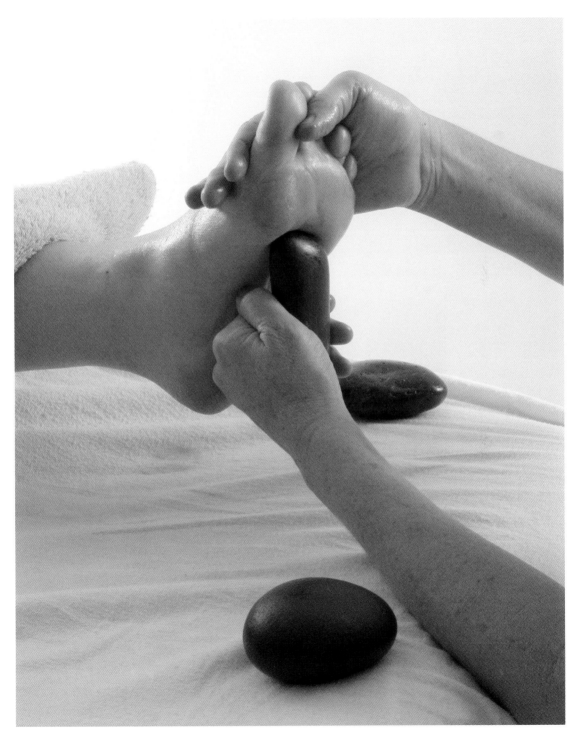

6. Apply massage cream to the recipient's hands and arms using effleurage strokes.

7. Use small round hot stones to massage the arms upward, toward the torso. Flip and replace stones often.

8. Remove the shoulder and neck stones and use small round hot stones to massage along the areas of tension. Follow with deep massage using your hands.

9. For the scalp and face, remove the stones so there is room for your hands and then massage the scalp and neck. For the facial massage, there are two options: warm stones are good for relieving sinus pressure and jaw pain; cool stones are good for relieving headache, toxicity, fatigue, and puffiness around the eyes.

RIGHT: **Step 10**

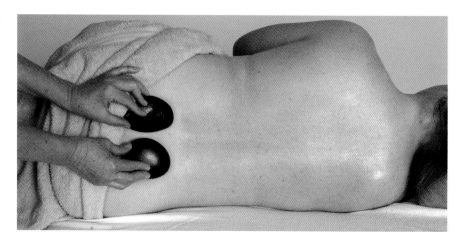

10. Have your recipient turn over to the side a little more, so that you can apply massage cream to her back. Apply the lubricant in broad, spreading effleurage strokes. You will work one side at a time. Be complete and include the sacral as well as the exposed side anatomy. Come up over the upper shoulder and onto the upper arm. Then, starting at the lower back, massage a heart shape with your stones over her back. Follow this with a slow-stroke, upward-moving spinal stone massage, drawing a smaller heart over the upper back. Finally, make your third heart-shaped stroke over the mid-thoracic area.

Return the stones to the warmer.

11. Select two new stones, and address the side of the body and the top of the upper shoulder. Rake hand-over-hand inward toward the midline. Repeat this several times. The moderate warmth of the stones will soften the tensions accompanying pregnancy. Here is an opportunity to perceive the quality of muscle tissue

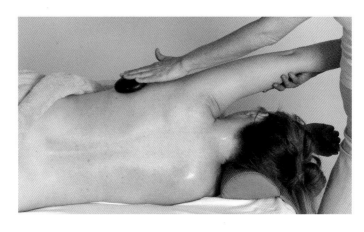

ABOVE: **Step 11**

through the stone, rather than feeling that the stone blocks your sensitivity.

Try this stretching massage combination: Walk to the head of the massage table and lift the recipient's arm over her head as you step away. This produces an elongating stretch. Invite her to inhale as you open the rib spaces in this way. Smooth out the extended side of her body as she exhales; this releases physical stress.

12. Follow this with massage down into the muscles between the shoulder blades and then along the arm to the hand. Here you will be decongesting and stimulating important energy lines, or meridians. Repeat the stretch and massage with your warm stone, beginning at the top of the shoulder. Rock back and forth over the recipient's

BELOW: **Step 12**

shoulder and then brush your stone down the arm, returning up to the shoulder.

Work the point, tip, or edge of your stone into the muscles along the spine, and attend to the lower back, where tension often collects during pregnancy. Keep in mind that prenatal massage considerations apply to this area too: do not use very deep pressure or high heat.

13. After you have completed the recipient's back, you can massage her legs. It will be a bit awkward to reach all surfaces in this position.

Move toward muscle groups in the buttocks and backside. Apply pressure from the hip down toward the left.

At the completion, ask the recipient to return to a more upright position so that you can close the treatment by giving a gentle stretch at the feet.

Allow your recipient to rest and renew for a few moments before getting up and getting dressed. Provide plenty of water for her to drink.

RIGHT: **Step 13**

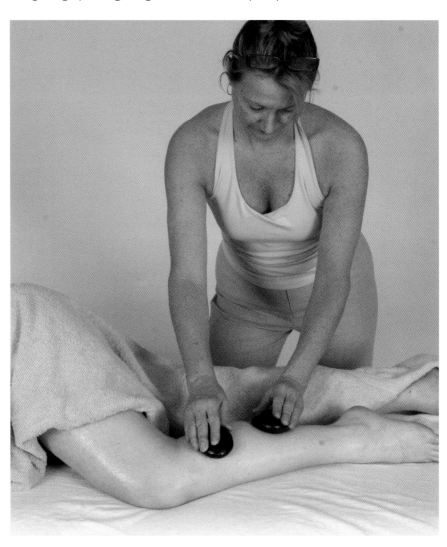

ATHLETE'S STONE MASSAGE: TAKING YOUR STONE MASSAGE DEEPER

Stone massage techniques can be especially effective in treating specific ailments or in facilitating certain types of activity. These techniques are an integral part of the training of stone massage practitioners and as such lie outside the scope of this book. To give the reader a general sense of the value of this kind of body-work, however, the following section on stone massage for athletes is included. You may find here suggestions that you can adapt to general massage sessions. If you wish to explore the subject in greater depth, please consult the references and bibliography at the back of the book.

Athlete's stone massage is based in classic Western massage. Some techniques are used more than others, depending on the situation and the desired results: compression with stones is often used to increase circulation in pre-event and post-event situations when athletes are clothed; while effleurage and petrissage with stones are performed in maintenance and recovery sessions where athletes are unclothed and draped, and cream is used on the skin.

Because of recurring stress, overload, and trauma to the body, athletes often need specific remedial work in their maintenance sessions. Athlete's stone massage practitioners should be skilled in locating and relieving trigger points, and in myofascial release techniques, which free the fascia and restore optimal mobility.

Techniques are often applied very specifically to certain muscles and tendons; therefore, athlete's stone massage specialists should have well-developed palpation skills and knowledge of musculoskeletal anatomy. Understanding the biomechanics of specific sports and fitness activities is also useful in planning sessions and in locating areas of bodily stress. Practitioners should be well-versed in the special needs of athletes and able to adapt massage sessions accordingly.

Let's look more closely at four aspects of sports massage.

RECOVERY

Assistance with recovery from strenuous exertion is a major application of sports massage. It addresses the tight, stiff, sore muscles that often accompany exercise, and helps the body heal minor tissue damage. For recovery, the practitioner spends time focused on the body areas most stressed during an athlete's performance—whether in an exercise regimen or competition.

Recovery massage generally includes techniques to improve circulation, promote muscular relaxation, and enhance flexibility. Effleurage, petrissage, and compression techniques are used to bring nutrients to an area, flush out metabolic waste products, and create hyperemia in a muscle group.

Joint mobilizations and jostling are used to help muscles relax and lengthen, and to release unconscious tension that may be held in the soft tissues. Broadening techniques are beneficial as well, helping to separate muscle fibers which can become adhered due to the stress of exercise.

An important component of recovery is relaxation. Warm stones help in the relaxation process and thereby promote healing.

REMEDIAL AND REHABILITATION MASSAGE

The remedial and rehabilitation applications of massage with athletes are the same as with other populations. The most common situations involve muscle tension and inflexibility, soreness, trigger points, edema, tendonitis, tenosynovitis, strains, sprains, and stress. Deep friction massage with heat and oil is especially useful in the development of healthy mobile scar tissue and in freeing adhesions after trauma.

MAINTENANCE

Maintenance is a term used to describe an all-purpose massage session that is received regularly and addresses specific needs. In maintenance sessions, you might focus on overall relaxation or on areas that are stressed from the recipient's sport or exercise routine. Maintenance sessions combine massage for recovery with massage for problem areas. Thermotherapy and deep tissue work with stones both amplify the effects of the maintenance massage.

EVENTS

The applications of massage at athletic events may be classified as either pre-event, inter-event, or post-event.

Pre-event massage is different from the other applications of sports massage outlined thus far. Developed to assist the athlete in preparing physically and mentally for an upcoming event, it is often part of the warm-up routine.

Pre-event massage lasts approximately fifteen to twenty minutes, is upbeat in tempo, and concentrates on the major muscle groups to be used in the upcoming performance. Relaxation may be required in cases of anxiety. This massage helps to increase psychological as well as physical readiness.

Inter-event massage is similar to pre-event and post-event massage but is performed between events at a competition. It also addresses recovery of the muscle groups used in performance as well as psychological readiness and recovery.

The primary goal of post-event massage is recovery, both physical and psychological. It also includes injury assessment, first aid, and referral to other health care practitioners.

GETTING STARTED: SPORTS MASSAGE WITH STONES

Here we will utilize your knowledge of stone massage to blend stone thermotherapy with sports massage in clinical applications such as pain and injury treatment, and post-event and maintenance work. A typical session begins with a foundation layout of warm stones.

As the athlete rests over the warm foundation stones, take his or her heels into your hands and gently lift and jostle the legs and spine. This creates a wavelike massage. Your own knees are unlocked and soft, your arms long, elbows stretched. Bring aware-ness to the ankles, the knees, and on up to the hips.

Isolate the athlete's hips one at a time, circling each femur in its joint capsule with slight traction. This should be very relaxing for the recipient, not vigorous. Centering is important in pre-event massage; your athlete can perform at his or her peak when focused, alert, and relaxed.

After completing the jostling and segmented assessment through the joints, re-drape both feet.

Now approach the left leg and undrape it. Tuck the towel snugly, exposing only the area receiving treatment. Take a hot stone into each hand. These stones should be able to remain comfortably on the skin for at least ten seconds. Make sure they are not too hot.

Allow the stones to become an extension of your hands. While the recipient is supine, apply alternating compression massage strokes to the thighs, calves, and hamstrings. Later when the recipient is prone, apply these strokes to the piriformis and gluteal muscle groups.

This aspect of the stone massage of the legs is aimed at warming and stimulating large muscles first, then the deeper small muscle groups. Experiment with different stone sizes and textures. Keep the heat consistent by flipping the stones frequently. When massaging the legs you may have success using large stones; they retain heat much longer than small ones.

Never combine Tiger Balm, menthol, camphor, eucalyptus or capsicum with heated stones, as this can burn the skin.

Remember, even though you are working with hotter stones than the ones in the foundation layout, the stones should not be too hot. The temperature should be tolerable to the skin for ten seconds or longer.

You need to repeat the massage with several passes over each area; otherwise the heat and energy of the stones won't penetrate into the deep tissue.

Make dynamic compressing movements with the hot stones in your palms, applying pressure in an anterior-to-posterior direction. Compression with heat begins to separate muscle fibers against the bone and increases nutritive hyperemia to the muscle groups. Don't bypass the delicate attachments around the knees, but be cautious. Use small stones for better access.

As you travel down to the ankle, change between ironing, pumping, and cross-fiber friction techniques with the stone, applying a combination of texture, heat, and pressure.

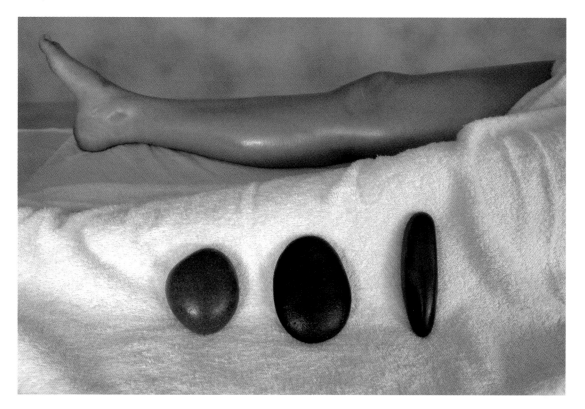

Sandwich the calf between your palm stones. Exert oscillating compression downward toward the foot. Keep your pressure firm and steady. Integrate the upper and lower leg work with broad spreading effleurage strokes.

Now apply compression. Use a firm, staccato, downward pumping movement on the hamstring muscles; as a result, fresh cleansing blood will flow through the fibers at a deep level. Lighten your pressure as you approach the vulnerable space behind the knee. Complete both legs in this manner.

When working on each foot, sandwich the ball of the foot between two stones. Gently jostle these joints and muscles with your warm stones. Consider the delicate skin on top of the foot, and work with a cooler, smoother stone there. These considerations always apply in stone massage; be especially careful when working over bony structures or directly on vulnerable skin such as the sacrum, belly, or top of the foot.

The "Waterfall" Stroke

The waterfall stroke is a stimulating upbeat movement that creates an aerobic vascular response and is good in pre-event sports massage.

It is accomplished by first applying massage cream manually with a deep tissue effleurage stroke, and then simultaneously massaging with one hot stone and one ice-cold stone along the direction of the muscle fiber. Use a firm, steady pace. The waterfall stroke is generally repeated three times to achieve the desired effect. Using thermotherapy in this way, you will open the pathway of venous circulation. This is the carrier of heat to an area of focus. Muscle nerves relax under the warm stone and then instantaneously contract due to the iced stone.

When you work on the small attachments around the knee, you may want to experiment with friction and with direct sustained holds at varying temperatures.

This technique registers differently with each person. Some athletes will say that they are able to distinguish the two contrasting temperatures; while others feel it like an "icy hot" sensation. It is invigorating and relaxing all at once.

The "Joint Sandwich"

Try the following technique for tendonitis, bursitis or sprains. Sandwich the joint between one warm (not hot) stone and one iced stone (of granite or quartzite) for sixty seconds. This effectively stimulates joint fluid movement in areas that are impossible to palpate.

Repeat the sequence, alternating the position of the hot and cold stones for sixty seconds at a time. Thermotherapy principles apply to this technique: the warmth is dilating—in this case, the synovial joint fluids expand—while the cold produces a sudden tonifying contraction. Polarity principles also come into play: the hot stone emits a positive ionic charge and the cold stone a negative charge. Directing such an exchange of opposite or attracting charges into an area of fluids is similar to magnet therapy.

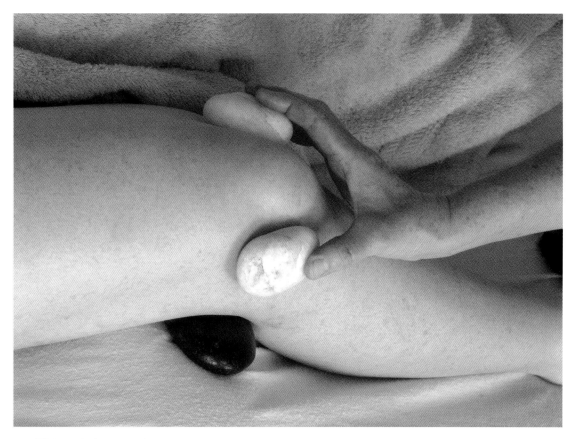

This technique can be applied to the shoulder, ankle, wrist, or any joint. The sequence is always the same. Start with a warm foundation stone positioned posteriorly and a cold one positioned anteriorly. The physical effect—the vascular response—is brought about by the transfer of heat and energy from warmer to colder locations.

ADDRESSING COMMON COMPLAINTS WITH STONE MASSAGE

SHOULDER TENSION

You will need at least three stones, two of which are flat and about two or three inches in diameter. Also you will need one or two point-work stones—long

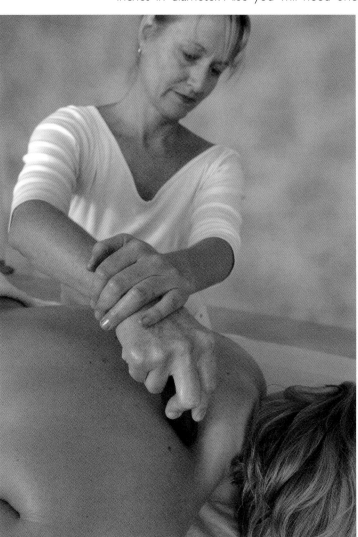

stones with a point on either end. Have extra stones nearby.

Prepare the upper body, shoulder and arm with warming stone massage. Apply an overhead arm stretch with one hot active stone, gliding it over the triceps muscle group. Repeat this several times. Follow this pattern with hot stone massage across and along the deltoid muscle fibers and their attachments at the rotator cuff. Be thorough, covering the entire shoulder girdle muscle group, including major and minor muscles.

Try a stretch with a stone in your hand for more dynamic effect. Cradling the elbow with your inside arm, exert a slight upward traction to the shoulder while applying direct, sustained pressure with a warm stone to the shoulder muscle, or over trigger points. Use your whole body and move from your feet for greater leverage. Follow any lines of tension you perceive beneath the stone; let this perception guide your work into deeper layers. Circling with the recipient's elbow bent helps to move muscle against the stone, while introducing warmth to the joint fluid.

Now, continuing into a deep shoulder release, walk around to the opposite side of table from the shoulder you are working on. As the picture shows, you may start out with a stone in your active hand and allow the less active hand to brace and cradle the shoulder and upper back. This hold helps expose the surface anatomy of the rhomboid, trapezius, and paraspinal muscles. In thermotherapy, shoulders can tolerate hotter stone temperatures than some other areas can. (As a general rule, any part of the body that is exposed to sunlight and that tans, is less sensitive to the hot stones. There are, however, always exceptions to this rule.) After several warming and elongating passes with a single stone, you might want to add a second stone in a raking hand-over-hand technique. End with your pointed stones for trigger point release.

TENNIS ELBOW

Warm the forearm by applying effleurage with hot stones and massage cream. Deepen your focus after each pass. Include both the anterior and posterior forearm, following the long muscles from wrist to elbow.

Apply deep circular friction to the attachments at the elbow, watching for bony prominences against your stone and adjusting your pressure as needed.

Next, hold the recipient's right hand below the wrist with your left hand. Place a cold white stone, approximately two inches long and as flat as possible for controlled placement, directly over the forearm muscle attachment atop the elbow. Press medially and firmly with your right thumb. Use deep pressure. Begin to step back, bringing the arm into a fascial stretch.

Now, slowly and without releasing the traction, rotate the hand first internally and then externally. Exert sustained, direct, deep medial pressure. Repeat this for three or four rotations. Be sure that the fingers of your right hand are comfortably placed around the recipient's forearm, with the pads rather than the points pressing into the arm.

Thermotherapy applications may alternate cold stones with warm stones. Since the stone will stay in one place for several minutes, the temperature must be warm rather than hot.

Without releasing the stone or the finger pressure draw the stone across the top of the attachment inward, rolling the muscle under the heat and pressure of the stone. You might choose the pointed end of a hot stone to focus on trigger point release here. Hold the stone for thirty seconds over each point. Following the hot pointed stone, apply an iced stone for thirty seconds or longer. Contrast thermotherapy will decongest metabolic waste buildup in this area.

CARPAL TUNNEL SYNDROME

For carpal tunnel and other wrist and hand treatments, place a large warm stone under the heel of the hand. Allow the stone below to support the extension at the wrist above.

Begin with a general warming massage of the arm by applying effleurage with hot stones and massage cream. Deepen your focus after each pass. Include the wrist, forearm, and hand, and follow the anatomy of the hand out to the tips of the fingers. Trace with a tiny warm stone along each finger, being mindful of the pressure. Follow with several integrating broad stretching strokes against a flat warm stone.

Next, sandwich the entire wrist between two flat warm stones. Find a comfortable holding spot on each of the two stones and then move forward and back. Your posture and movements may feel like Tai Chi or a dance.

This movement provides gentle mobilization to the joints of the wrist, elbow and shoulder. It also helps to open the lung meridian.

Remember to move through the natural range of motion, beginning with complete external rotation and proceeding with internal rotation and abduction. Do these movements three to six times or until the stones lose their warmth. Feel free to integrate modalities such as jostling or deeper connective tissue mobilization. When you complete this technique gently lift off the hand, leaving the base stones.

ATHLETE'S STONE MASSAGE SUMMARY

Athlete's stone massage is most effective when basic thermal therapies are combined with massage techniques for specific conditions. Trigger point therapy, myofascial techniques, and deep transverse friction are especially useful in combination with ice and heat. Flat stone compressions are frequently used at athletic events since athletes typically remain clothed at such events.

It is possible to bring stones to a sport event. You may want to limit your selection to about six or eight specialty stones, and to focus the stone massage on small layouts only. The stones may fit into a pocket of the massage table travel case, or inside a canvas tote bag. To warm the stones on site, pack a small ten- or twelve-inch electric skillet, or submerge the stones in a sink filled with very hot water for ten minutes.

Healing Earth and Healing Clay Baths

HEALING CLAYS have been used as part of natural medicine for thousands of years, for internal detoxification of the digestive system and liver; relief of skin conditions; and organ and elimination system stimulation. Today, healing clays are used around the world in hydrotherapy, balneology, natural medicine, and alternative medicine.

Clay baths are a fantastic way to help relieve stress and relax, especially in the evening before bed. Clay baths support the metabolic processes of the body. By stimulating the lymphatic system and by taking part of the burden from the organs of elimination, they can greatly improve one's health and sense of well-being. Modern research has shown that the people of some cultures greatly benefit from ingesting clays as a natural ingredient in their water supplies.

Today the beneficial qualities of bentonite for industrial and cosmetic use are widely recognized. Though known primarily for its use in luxurious facial cosmetics in France, at one time clay was used by French sailors to prevent dysentery: they added it to their drinking water supply. Indeed, bentonite will inoculate water contaminated with a very wide variety of bacteria, rendering it safe to drink.

TAKING A HEALING CLAY BATH

Taking a therapeutic clay bath lasting from fifteen minutes to two hours is one of the most effective methods there is to assist the body in eliminating toxic substances that have accumulated. Clay baths stimulate the lymphatic system and deeply cleanse the body's largest breathing organ, the skin. Used in this manner, clay interacts directly with the immune system and also helps to remove the post-digestive burden placed on the major organs of the body.

Taking a clay bath is like immersing in a sea of millions of minute crystals. A healing clay bath should predominantly consist of green bentonites (low-sodium or high-sodium) and montmorillonites. Natural raw clays are best.

Pay careful attention when storing clay: store it in a completely sealed container, away from petroleum chemicals. Do not allow clay to come in prolonged contact with metals. If it is necessary to store clay in plastic, the best choice is FDA-grade plastic.

When buying clays for long-term and regular clay baths, consider matters of cost and convenience. Ten cups of clay added to a bath has proven to be effective. No less than four cups of clay should be used in a standard bath; preferably, eight to ten. Ideally, between four and ten pounds of clay should be used in a bath that is deep enough to comfortably and completely submerge the body.

Given modern plumbing, and pipes in good shape—not clogged—clay will not stick to the pipes and cause problems as long as it is completely aqueous when drained. You may, however, need to take extra precautions if you have a septic system. The sandy silt that may be left behind from a clay bath poses no problem.

It is best to begin with tepid or warm clay baths between ninety-eight and one hundred degrees. That means that the water temperature is either slightly warm to the touch, or there is no feeling of a temperature difference.

First, measure out the amount of clay to be used in the bath. Then put this clay into a large ceramic or glass container. Add five to six times the water by volume, and allow the clay to completely hydrate. You can mix it with a non-metal stirring device. By pre-preparing the clay in this manner, it will quickly combine when added to the bath, without clumping. You will also avoid adding clay dust to the air.

Turn on the hot water, and secure the plug. As the water enters the tub, add the clay, filling the tub only enough to comfortably submerge your entire body. If the clay settles at the bottom of the tub, a few short moments of agitation will suffice. One to five cups of quality sea salt may be added to any clay bath.

The average "standard" duration of a clay bath is twenty to thirty minutes. To start, however, try fifteen minutes. Slowly increase the amount of time spent in the bath as you can tolerate it. The body will, over time, allow more substances to be released. After ten or fifteen minutes the internal body temperature will begin to rise. This produces a therapeutic effect.

FIELD GUIDE TO HEALING CLAYS

No two clays are the same.

A healing clay bath should predominantly consist of green sodium smectite. This includes swelling bentonites (low-sodium or high-sodium) and montmorillonites. Fifty to seventy-five percent swelling green clay is recommended for clay baths. Natural, raw clays are best; agricultural grade clays are next best; and technical grade clays are third.

AMERICAN COLLOID HPM-20

This is an exceptional agricultural-certified Wyoming clay that is processed to "technical standards," or via air purification. This clay has a ph of 8.5-10, and fully dispersed has a surface area of greater than seven hundred fifty square meters per gram. It has 2.7% magnesium, 2.4% sodium, and 1.3% calcium. The average particle size is five microns in diameter.

GREEN WYOMING BENTONITES

These have proven to be excellent for bath use.

UTAH BENTONITE

Utah bentonite blended with Wyoming bentonite makes an acceptable blend of green smectites.

REDMOND CLAY

Marketed by Real Salt, this is also an excellent clay to add to green bentonite.

BIBLIOGRAPHY

Ackerman, Diane. *A Natural History of the Senses*. Random House, 1990.

Anthony, Carol. *Guide to the I Ching*. Anthony Publishing Company, 1982.

Barral, Dr. Jean-Pierre. *Visceral Manipulation*. Eastland Press, 1989.

Campbell, Joseph. *Myths to Live By*. Viking Press, 1972.

Chia, Mantak and Tao Huang. *The Secret Teachings of the Tao Te Ching*. Destiny Books, 2005.

Chopra, Dr. Deepak. *The Book of Secrets: Unlocking the Hidden Dimensions of Your Life*. Harmony Books, 2004.

Conway, D.J. *Laying on of Stones*. Ten Speed Press, 2001.

Cunningham, Scott. *Cunningham's Encyclopedia of Crystal, Gem, and Metal Magic*. Llewellyn Publications, 2000.

Dasgupta, Surendrenath. *Natural Science of the Ancient Hindus*. Indian Council of Philosophical Research, 1987.

Dash, Vaidya Bhagwan. *Massage Therapy in Ayurveda*. Concept Publishing, 2002.

Earth Prayers from Around the World. Edited by Elizabeth Roberts and Elias Amidon. HarperSanFrancisco, 1991.

Finlay, Victoria. *Color, A Natural History of the Palette*. Ballantine Books, 2002.

Frawley, David. *From the River of Heaven*. Book Passage Press, 1990.

Gerber, Dr. Richard. *Vibrational Medicine: New Choices for Healing Ourselves*. Bear & Co., 1998.

Huang, Alfred. *The Complete I Ching: The Definitive Translation*. Inner Traditions, 1998.

Iyengar B.K.S. *Light on the Yoga Sutras of Patanjali*. Aquarian, 1993.

Kaptchuk, Ted. *The Web That Has No Weaver: Understanding Chinese Medicine*. Congdon & Weed, 1983.

Lad, Vasant Dattatray. *Textbook of Ayurveda, Fundamental Principles*. Ayurvedic Press, 2002.

Miller, Dr. Light and Dr. Bryan Miller. *Ayurveda and Aromatherapy*.

Murphy, Joseph. *Special Meditations for Health, Wealth, Love and Expression*. DeVorss & Company, 1979.

Olsen, Andrea. *Bodystories*. Station Hill Press, 1991.

Panikkar, Raimundo. *The Vedic Experience; Mantramanjari*. University of California Press, 1977.

Pitchford, Paul. *Healing with Whole Foods*. North Atlantic Books, 2002.

Shumsk, Susan G. *Chakras Coloring Book*.

Svoboda, Dr. Robert and Arnie Lade. *Tao and Dharma*. Lotus Press, 1995.

Svoboda, Dr. Robert. *Ayurveda for Women*. Healing Arts Press, 2000.

Teeguarden, Iona. *The Joy of Feeling, Bodymind Acupressure.*. Japan Publications, 1987.

Thorson, Robert M. *Stone by Stone; The Magnificent History of New England Stone Walls*. Walker & Co. 2002.

Upledger, Dr. John. *A Brain is Born*. North Atlantic Books, 1996.

Vedic Culture. Edited by Stephen Knapp. IUniverse, 2005.

Walker, Brian Browne. *The I Ching or Book of Changes*. St. Martin's Press, 1992.

RESOURCE GUIDE

STONE MASSAGE SUPPLIERS

Stone Temple LLC
www.stonetempleinstitute.com
860 395-1954

RECOMMENDED HEALING STONE THERAPY EDUCATION AND INSTRUCTORS

Stone Temple Institute
Po Box 820
Essex, CT 06426
DIRECTOR: **Carollanne Vedi Crichton LMT**
www.stonetempleinstitute.com
Email: info@healingstonemassage.com
860 395-0282

Sarah Maxwell LMT
Smax2@comcast.net
860 669-2548

Swedish Institute
26 W. 26th St.
New York, NY 10026
212 924-5900
INSTRUCTOR: **Jeannine Hamel–Smith LMT**
860 395-0440

Carol Joy Campbell LMT
Caroljoy33@yahoo.com
508 285-8840

Jerri Levine LMT
Twin Falls, ID
Blue_lotus1@netzero.com

Edward Massee LMT
Aurora, IL
630 897-7655

Debbe Bond LMT
Tybee Island, GA
relaxfirst@bellsouth.net

Cindilee Ecker-Flagg
Toronto Area, Ontario Canada
905 899-0450
www.thesacredplacewithinjourneybegins.com

Edith Dore LMT DAc
Mountain Home, AK
edith@webewireless.com
870 425-2311

George Swainston LMT
Reno, NV
rubman@aol.com

Institute for Integrative Healthcare Seminars
Natural Wellness
Pine Bush, NY
www. NaturalWellness.com

Real Bodywork Training Videos
Santa Barbara, CA
805 555-5511
ww.realbodywork.com

PHOTO CREDITS

© Bill Nelson pp. 34, 35, 46, 47, 125, 144, 161-163, 164 (top), 166, 168-174, 181

© Nancy Dionne pp. 106, 110, 112, 116, 126, 131, 145, 148,150, 152, 155, 157-159, 164 (bottom), 165, 177-179, 182, 183

p. 8 © Arlene Gee, p. 13 © Maartje van Caspel, p. 14 © Chris Gates, p. 17 © Sean Locke,
p. 18 ©Andrea Gingerich, p. 22 © Kevin Drinkall, p. 25 ©Wouter van Caspel, p. 26 © Kyle Maass,
p. 29 © Mark Atkins, p. 31 (all), 33, 44-45, 61, 62, 64 courtesy of the Bridgeman Art Library,
p. 37 © Don Wilkie, p. 38 University of Zurich, pp. 40-41, 91 & 93 © Mike Morley p. 48 © Christian Sawicki,
pp. 50 & 53 © Kelly Cline, p. 54 Shasti O'Leary-Soudant, p. 56 © Lise Gagne, p. 57 © Oleg Prikhodko,
p. 58 © Daniel Brunner, p. 73 © Christopher North, p. 75 © Ryan Fardo, p. 77 © René Mansi,
p. 78 © Anssi Ruuska, p. 79 ©Mtain, p. 80 © Bodgan, p. 84 ©Thomas Winstead, p. 88 © Paige Foster,
p. 90 © Goran Zakula, p. 92 © Harry Thomas, p. 96 © Filipe Wiens, p. 97 © Roger Pilkington,
pp. 98-101 (all) © Irmin Eitel, p. 104 © Shaun Lowe, p. 108 © Lynn Watson, p. 113 ©Vera Bogaert,
p. 120 © Marje Cannon (bottom), p. 120(top), 128 © Luca di Filippo, p. 122 © Matthew Scherf,
p. 123 © Juergen Sack, p. 132 Luc Gillet, p. 134 © James Boulette, p. 137 © Peter Nguyen,
p. 139 Martin Heijkenskjöld, p. 141 © Justin Horrocks, p. 186 © Alija

NOTES

1. Lao Tzu. *Tao Te Ching, Book of the Way.* Translation Stephen Mitchell. HarperCollins, 1988.

2. Braden, Gregg. *The God Code: The Secret of Our Past, the Promise of Our Future.* Hay House, 2004.

3. Grey Wolf, *Native American Widsom.* Judy Piatkus Publisher, 2000.

4. Gach, Michael Reed. *Acupressure's Potent Points : A Guide to Self-Care for Common Ailments.* Bantam Books, 1990.